'I have gone from dinghy to ocean yacht, from picnic on Snowdon to oxygen on Manaslu, from bushcraft in Dorset to Borneo jungle, but not by any particularly adventurous routes, and none of them extraordinary.

I've got good at getting better at things, by gradually pushing boundaries, challenging and learning; and thereby, I've got better at being me – knowing myself, understanding what's important to me, being clear on my values and principles. The wild has been my companion and my stimulus on my two journeys; in particular, the internal journey I have been on. I have come a long way from that shy, risk-averse teenager.'

Paul Samuel

Find
Your Own
Mountains

Paul Samuel

First published in 2018 by Ana Lesiak Samuel

ISBN 978-1-911195-90-0

Also available as an ebook

ISBN 978-1-911195-91-7

Typeset by Jill Sawyer

Cover design by Alice Moore

Printed and bound by Clays, St Ives

Prologue

Find Your Own Mountains is Paul's first book. He had plans for other ones. But he was not given the opportunity to write them. On 30 June 2018, several weeks after completing the final draft of *Find Your Own Mountains*, my beloved husband Paul perished in an avalanche on his attempt to summit Alpamayo, one of the most beautiful mountains in the world.

Henry Miller once said: 'No man would set a word down on paper if he had the courage to live out what he believed in…' and 'The truly great writer does not want to write. He wants the world to be a place in which he can live the life of the imagination.' Paul did both – he lived the life he set out for himself and he became a writer.

Although his story was finished prematurely, Paul lived a hundred times the life of most people. He was the most loving husband, deeply dedicated father and very caring son. A valedictorian with a First in Classics from the University of Cambridge and a Dean's list award from INSEAD Business School, he became a successful entrepreneur and an inspiring boss, mentor and colleague. While working on his ongoing and new business ventures, he managed to sail half of the world in the Clipper Round the World Race, pull sleighs to the South Pole, explore the jungles of Borneo and the wilderness of Nova Scotia, and climb a number of the highest mountains in the world.

A man of noble humility, Paul deeply touched and inspired people around him. Described as 'a gentleman explorer' by Discovery Channel in their footage of his team's Everest attempt, Paul was a gentleman in every sense of the word – a quality that seems rare these days. A rock to count on, with an incredibly generous heart and virtuous modesty, he gave without any expectation of reciprocity. He had a remarkable moral code and integrity of character. Accompanied by eloquence and courage, this was the trait that set him apart. It was his incredible talent, enormous character and the desire to work hard to excel that made him not only a high achiever but also an amazing husband, father, friend, mentor and boss. He left the world a better place than when he entered it.

Ana

This book is a series of 18 letters to my daughter, Kate, based on notes in diaries and letters written during some of my adventures.

Manaslu, camp 2, 6,400 metres
16 September 2013

I looked over to Louis, my climbing buddy; we had just carried up our high-altitude gear, jumaring up ropes put in earlier by our Sherpa support team, at times dodging crevasses, at others going knee-deep in drift snow. We had boiled and forced down our dehydrated meals and the weather was closing in. I was still shivering from navigating the snowy winds outside our tent in my head torch for evening ablutions. The dark skies were freezing around us and the bumpy ice under my sleeping mat presaged an uncomfortable night. Intermittent sleep, wild dreams and showers of ice crystals from our frozen breathing certainly lay ahead.

'Why the **** do we do this, Louis?' I asked.

'You're right, mate,' he said in his Afrikaans drawl, 'we're getting too old for this shit.'

***

'Every man is tasked to make his life, even in its details, worthy of the contemplation of his most elevated and critical hour.'

Henry David Thoreau, *Walden; or, Life in the Woods*

My Dear Kate,

I set up a new business two months after you were born.

I had planned it and had set aside money for it and I was in a determined mood, after the previous few years. But your arrival forced some reflection.

While you were breastfeeding I would come to visit at the weekends but as soon as you were on the bottle, I agreed with your mum that I could have you every other weekend. I think that was scarier at first than starting the business. It was the first time I had felt the responsibility of someone or something totally dependent on me with no means of mutual communication. But we didn't need to. The times we had really felt like it was you and me in it together; you were a distraction but also a motivation. You helped me get that business going and that bond has helped me over other waters since.

Eight months later, I headed to Bolivia, to the mountains. They seemed more important than ever.

In this book, I want to explain why.

From that trip on, I started writing notes and letters for you in my diaries; this book is a distillation of those and of some of the adventures themselves. The experiences from them have been much of the inspiration and schooling for shaping who I am today, and for the letters I write to you here.

What do I hope you get from this book?

A passion for life; an appreciation of its worth and from that, I hope, a desire to make the most out of it. You might think this an obvious aspiration; it is likely you haven't thought much about it to date. Why would you?

But I hope you reflect on it as you go through life. There are many challenges that can deflect from its fulfilment. When you hear yourself saying 'Life goes so fast' or 'Where has the time gone?' or similar, then I hope you will turn to this book and its reflections. We are currently only on this Earth for around 1,000 months on average, and you are potentially around a fifth of your way through that already, Kate. It is in your power to make the rest of your time as fast or as slow as you want.

You're about to step out into the world. Much of your journey to date has been laid out for you; now the canvas is your own. That is the challenge and the joy of existence. You can let life come to you or you can be proactive about living it to the full. The prize and the spur is you yourself, and, as Thoreau says, the reflections of your finest hour. That is worth consciously fighting for.

I hope this book will be something you dip into over time. While I am sure you would have worked out much by yourself, on your own journey, I hope this will provide some pointers and references, maybe some shortcuts and nudges, and, if it doesn't actually stop you falling down some of the same holes as I have, at least it will tell you that you're not alone in so doing.

I look forward to watching you on your journey and to sharing more experiences with you along the way. Whatever you take from this book, know that I am there always for you, whether that's an ear when you need to talk, a shoulder when you need support, or advice when you are stuck or unsure.

I am extremely proud of you, Kate. Know that the light you gave me when you first came into this world remains undimmed.

Happy Birthday!

With my love always,
Dad xx

Contents

***

I quote from a few authors in the book, so I have attached a brief description of the more prominent ones at the end of the book, alongside a short suggested reading list.

1. Stepping Out

Canada and USA
Feb–July 1982

How to Keep Your Volkswagen Alive: A Manual of Step by Step Procedures for the Compleat Idiot

I opened the book and chuckled, 'That's the one for me.'

How naivety can trump stupidity.

I had hatched a cunning plan. It was to spend a lot of my gap year earnings on a VW Beetle to drive around America. Beetles were pretty simple cars, right?

All I had when I landed in Vancouver on a grey morning in February 1982 was a ticket out from Toronto five months later and a bed and offer of work from some generous friends of my parents, Noel and Valerie. They picked me up from the airport and drove me to their home in a small agricultural community called Ladner and, while I worked in their fertiliser business, living in the comfort of their outside cabin, I developed my plan to storm the States by car. The US didn't look that big on the map laid out on my bed.

As I set off on my quest, waving goodbye from my Beetle window, a clapped-out radio for company, my suitcase and an old cooler with some food in the back seat, I wrote:

And so the beginning – I'm still not sure whether I have realised what I'm doing and am about to face. I feel a bit pathetic – so many people have done this before so I'm nobody special.

Today was the big day of breaking with family life and protection. I'm writing this from a parking lot in Princeton, a small town up in the Rockies I suppose about 200 miles east of Vancouver. It was a hard drive but the views are fantastic. I suppose it is my smallness and lack of someone to lean on. Noel and Valerie were so good to me, it was really sad to leave them, also considering what is in front of me.

I don't know what I will do tonight – maybe keep driving till I get tired.

I parked up, got my tent out, rolled out my mat and sleeping bag and looked out into the silent air. Was this how it was going to be for the next three and a half months?

Toronto, 16 July
One week to go! I feel like I'm just about ready for it, though I know that once I get back home, I'll be wanting to come back again.

'Boy to man' was how I later described the experience to people. What happened on that trip around the USA?

***

Los Angeles, 3 June 1982
1 a.m., downtown Greyhound station

'Excuse me,' I say, as I try to get by; I don't want to catch him with my backpack frame. A giant, leaning against the restroom door entrance with his arms crossed, he straightens and looks down at me, a bit bemused or sleepy, I can't really tell. Still, I need to go to the loo and I have a bus to Las Vegas to catch. Inside, there are half a dozen of his friends just hanging around, leaning against walls, making small talk that I can't understand but don't really listen to. The conversation stops as I walk to the urinals.

Strange place to meet your mates for a chat, I think to myself, but whatever. I turn my back to them. The only sound is me urinating... and then washing my hands. I smile briefly at one of them on my way out and leave the guy at the door behind; he has now woken up a bit but still looks confused.

I hand my ticket over to the Greyhound driver, put my pack in the hold, and mount the steps of the bus for what tomorrow will bring. What a couple of weeks.

It had started with me on the side of a road in Yosemite National Park. I had long since realised that America was a lot bigger than I had anticipated and I was already thinking that my ambitions to cross the country by car might be a bit hopeful. Then it started heating up on the moderate hills of Yosemite. I was also realising that the 'idiot's guide' to car maintenance had its limits – or maybe I did.

Time for a rethink. Rather than going on to LA, I got to a phone box.

'Louise?' I pushed in the quarter as the phone beeped. 'Hi, it's Paul. How are you?'

After pleasantries, I got to the point:

'I was wondering if you would mind me coming back to San Francisco to stay for a bit longer? I'm going to try to sell the car.'

Louise was another generous soul, a friend of a friend, who had agreed by letter to help me out if I was passing through San Fran. Here I was, imposing again; but she sounded genuine in her 'No problems', back down the line.

As I flicked through her local newspaper to look for price comparatives, I came across a cartoon with a cat in it; I chuckled and Louise looked over.

'Funny, eh? You can get mugs and everything with him on these days.'

While I waited for calls to view the car, I went shopping for a backpack and, sure enough, there in a shop window were rows of orange stuffed cats.

I got the telephone number via a label and made a call when I got back to Louise's.

'Hello, I'm calling about Garfield.' I tried to deepen my voice. 'I'm from the UK and I am enquiring about the distribution rights. Are they available?'

I wasn't sure what I was going to do with them, as I was off to university, but I'd worry about that later.

One of the reasons I'd come to America was for inspiration. People talked about it as the land of opportunity, a 'can do' place; and it was true. The country buzzed with energy. Maybe some of that had rubbed off.

After some passing around, a lady finally said, 'I'm sorry sir, they have already been taken.'

I thanked her and resumed my repacking. That solves that one, I said to myself.

My luck was that Louise lived a mile from one of the richest universities in the country, and Beetles still had a Californian coolness to them. So even though mine was a little beaten-up and had British Columbia number plates, I got more for the car than I had paid for it.

All of a sudden, I had transferred all my kit from an unruly spread across the back of the car to the front drive of Louise's house. I filled my backpack; what didn't fit had to go. In a few days, I went from car and tenting to bus and hostelling.

It changed my life.

Getting out of the closet of the car altered the dynamics of my trip completely. I had to talk to my neighbours, and once I started to talk, it nearly always led somewhere. I met people with such varied backgrounds, dreams and perspectives, but all with a common interest at that one point in time; there were always things to talk about, even if it was just swapping stories and advice or recommendations. From this common point, all sorts of discussions came about…

People are in transit. They are there to experience, see and learn, and this fosters an overall interest in others' perspectives. My diary changes much from San Francisco onwards; I rely less and less on calling people for a bed and more and more on finding my own way. Increasingly, people of different nationalities and different points in life come into the text. They brought huge colour to my trip. It was an explosion of experiences every day; not just amazing places but the variety of people. I had had a lid lifted.

***

'The bigger you make your world, the bigger it will make you.'

My diaries, Antarctica 2005

'Twenty years from now you will be more disappointed by the things that you didn't do than by the ones you did do.'

Attributed to Mark Twain

Dear Kate,

I wonder how you'll feel as you get closer to heading out on your gap year. It is a big symbolic event, leaving the bubble of home, school and local life for the first time.

I don't know what you see in me when you look at me today, but what I am now is not what I was when I was your age. If I seem reasonably together and comfortable in my own skin now, then it is a result of a lot of bumps and blind alleys on the journey, as well as, of course, many great experiences. When I was at your age, I was as green as a Cheshire field in spring; between an insulated school life, a stable home on a farm and most of my holidays being in North Wales (and no overseas visit further than Ibiza), I hadn't seen much of the world physically and I had no worldliness about me.

I was very shy; parties were often hard for me unless I knew everyone, and approaching girls was the hardest thing without Claire to help. I was confident enough in what I knew or could do but wouldn't willingly try something new; if I had to, I would certainly give it a good go, but I needed leading or pushing into anything that I didn't feel comfortable with. I think that is one of the reasons I bought the car; it was a kind of protection or layer between me and the outside world so when I shed it, many things changed.

My time in the States was an eye-opener on much and launch pad for more. The single biggest learning was that my life was up to me. It sounds obvious but when I was on my own, it really brought it home. Where I went each day, how I went about it and how I responded to all the unforeseen situations I found myself in, that was my call. Nothing happened without me making a conscious decision to do it.

When she was eighteen, Dame Ellen MacArthur sailed solo around Britain in her boat *Iduna*.

'I grew up on that trip around Britain... I forced myself to make decisions which I'd never taken before. I had sole responsibility for myself and for every move we made. I know now that there are no magic methods for making a situation better, you just have to stay calm, do all you can and believe that things will improve. You can't really anticipate that feeling sitting at home alone. It's not just the fact that you're on your own, but the safety decisions; do I go or do I wait? There is never an unquestionably right answer – except of course with hindsight.'

'I have no choice...' is a phrase said sometimes to try to justify a position or a path, sometimes to avoid responsibility or blame. But when I went round the States, I realised a situation might be someone else's fault, or just some bad luck, or random event, but so what? What was I going to do about it? The car was overheating in the middle of California, 10,000 miles to go. If that were to happen again on a road in the middle of Nevada, I could be in trouble. I had to make a decision. It gets even clearer when you're out in nature. The autopilot has gone on the blink in the middle of the North Sea? Fix it or find a way round it but doing nothing is not an option. '*I grew to realise that there is no one to blame*', as MacArthur says.

It is the difference between being a driver or a passenger in life. The driver has to be continuously aware of what is happening around her and make decisions as matters arise; the journey may be planned but any manner of things can happen unexpectedly during the trip. The driver will be able to recall many features of the route and probably retrace the journey without need for maps.

A passenger, on the other hand, rarely can recall the route or the journey; he has passed the responsibility for the trip to another.

I learnt in the US to accept that we have choice at any moment and that it is our responsibility what choices we make, even or especially if it is just carrying on as is. Not making a decision is still making a decision. And when we make decisions to do things (however big or small), we are taking control of our life. Give up or not accept that freedom of choice or personal responsibility and our existence is diminished. The actual understanding that our life is up to us, that we make of it what we will, is an incredible life-affirming force when we actually 'do things'.

Stepping out on your own for the first time is daunting. It was for me. I hope you don't wander into strange restrooms, but you are likely to make some strange decisions, with hindsight. But that is how you learn. If you stick with it, it will provide a richness and dimension you have yet to see and yield rewards that Croesus could not match. It will make you a bigger person.

With love,
Dad xx

2. Know Yourself

'Cholera?' I repeated the word back to the receptionist at the Hotel Oxford in a raised voice. I looked at Nick. I wasn't sure if he was going to laugh, cry or attack the guy.

'You mean where we were staying two weeks ago, that floor has been shut off because of suspected cholera?' Nick followed up.

The man nodded.

I started to laugh. And shake my head at the same time.

***

Three weeks earlier, we had landed at Cairo airport, from Athens – my first trip to the country of my most formative education. We'd toured the land of the Oracle and the Olympic Games, and, of course, the home of democracy, the city of the greatest learning, literature and architecture of the fifth century BC: Athens, home to giants like Socrates, Euripides and Aristotle.

But Cairo was something different. Nick had picked up on the plane an American travelling alone, who quickly became known as Wild Bill to us. He had a brown goatee, a permanent red bandana and an easy-going smile. We piled into a taxi and I directed the driver to the Hotel Oxford. The guidebook said it was central and cheap. The car weaved through traffic, broken-down buses, potholes and cattle-drawn carts, dust clouds stopping us opening any windows for respite from the stifling thirty-plus heat outside.

We got a room for three. Dirty paint was peeling from the walls; the windows, blackened by the traffic outside, refused to open; and the fan high up on the ceiling had cobwebs on it.

'Woah, I'm not using these sheets,' said Bill, picking up the corner of one disparagingly.

'Yup, sleeping bag time,' added Nick.

'What do you expect for two dollars a night, boys?' I rejoined. It was a bed, right?

We headed into the late afternoon bustle for food. And that was my next mistake; I hadn't yet learnt not to eat meat in such places, and I paid for it that night, dodging cockroaches in and around the loo on multiple occasions.

We all swore we'd never come back to the place as we headed south to Luxor and Aswan. Southern Egypt was a feast for the eyes, if not the belly still, the majesty of the temples of Luxor, the wonder of the Valley of the Kings, wobbly donkey rides over the hills and a seven-day felucca sail up the Nile to Aswan. We were very chilled as we jumped the train back to Cairo, in the late afternoon dust of Aswan. Third class? Why not. No seat reservations? It looked pretty empty. No food or drink? There's bound to be some on the train, and anyway we get in to Cairo for breakfast so we can treat ourselves there.

It was all going to plan till we got kicked out of our seats at the next station along the way, with no further seats available. People were already standing in the aisles.

'There's some space between these carriages,' I said to Nick and Bill.

It looked OK. We found some empty Coke crates and sat down on them, our backpacks to one side. The train bumped slowly along the tracks and we bounced along on the crates. Then the toilet door not far away swung open and a terrible smell wafted out. The toilet was an inch deep in liquid and the door wouldn't reclose.

Two locals came to sit down opposite us in their robes and scarved headgear, their cragged moustached faces nodding as they lowered themselves. These blonde lads in shorts opposite them must have seemed an oddity.

I looked at Nick and he shrugged. The night wore on and the train continued its crawl. I dozed in small stretches till the next jolt shot my head backwards, or the toilet door slammed nearby. Until I woke to find one of the Arabs touching my hair. I think it was more out of curiosity, but I let him know; and of course that was the end of my sleeping for the journey.

I wandered up the train to find some food, and wandered back down having found none. The Coke we had brought was all we had. Still, we'd be in Cairo for breakfast; I was clinging to that thought, and we'd promised ourselves a better hotel too. Clean sheets and a shower? That lifted my mind from our predicament.

The Arab kept looking elsewhere. Eight o'clock came and the train was still in open countryside; ten, twelve, no word of course, and we were now eighteen hours without food or water. Finally, at two the city sprawl started to appear and by four we were getting off the train.

'Let's get the hotel sorted first, boys,' Nick said, as we grabbed bottles of Coke from a station vendor. We had already agreed a list of five prospects in the book. I got into the front of the taxi and pointed to the first one in the book.

'Can't wait for a shower.' Bill was lifting his shirt from his body; the bandana, though, still stuck to his neck.

'I'm starving.' I looked back at the others. 'We're going somewhere decent tonight, right, guys?'

We got to the hotel. 'Wait here, boys. I'll go in and check,' I said. Full.

'Great!' Nick shrugged. 'OK, let's try number two.'

Full. And the next one, and the one after that, and the one after that. It was now six o'clock. We had no beds still and we hadn't eaten for twenty-six hours.

We looked at each other, not wanting to be the first one to say it. 'Hotel Oxford?'

***

'I am not yet able, as the Delphic inscription has it, to know myself; so it seems to me ridiculous, when I do not yet know that, to investigate irrelevant things.'

Socrates, in Plato's *Phaedrus*

'"I have begun to be a friend to myself." That was indeed a great benefit ... You may be sure that such a man is a friend to all mankind.'

Seneca, *Ad Lucilium Epistulae Morales* VI.7

Dear Kate,

While Egypt was a more eventful part of that trip than Greece, the time in the home of my schooling was equally impactful, just in a different way. It gave me my first glimpse at the relics of my imagination. Even though I walked among ruins, I felt like I knew their secrets and their stories; I felt like I was sharing many of the places with the ghosts of my books.

'Know yourself' was a phrase inscribed at the entrance to Apollo's temple at Delphi, the home of the Oracle and High Priestess Pythia, whom all Greeks over centuries looked to for prophecy and direction. For Socrates, as he says above, the saying was a key life imperative.

The Oracle is said to have said there was no one wiser than Socrates; his response, in Plato's *Apology*, was '*when I heard this, I thought to myself: "What in the world does the god mean, and what riddle is he propounding? For I am conscious that I am not wise either much or little. What then does he mean by declaring that I am the wisest?"*'

So then, '*with great reluctance I proceeded to investigate*'. He says he went to talk to a supposedly wise man in Athens, after which he had to conclude that '*neither of us really knows anything fine and good, but this man thinks he knows something when he does not, whereas I, as I do not know anything, do not think I do either. I seem, then, in just this little thing to be wiser than this man at any rate, that, what I do not know, I do not think I know either.*'

'Knowing yourself' has been a challenge for over 2,500 years, and even the great Socrates said he couldn't crack it. What's it all about?

Socrates said on another occasion that the unexamined life was not worth living. I agree. It's the principle of establishing truth in life. And that starts with us. This is what Socrates was getting at – the path to greater knowledge starts with acknowledging ignorance; if we live in false realities, then we have no chance of discovering truths. It is an important principle, especially in today's world.

We live increasingly online. Pressure prevails to be a part, to comment, to like and be liked. Media ideals are all around and their influence is so pervasive and invasive that self-definition is more at risk of being derived or heavily influenced from external sources than in the past. What is real and what isn't? Fake news, selfies, touch-ups; self-image can seem more important than self-awareness.

We can become people that we aren't or chase aspirations we've absorbed from others or online. What is the real 'me' versus me as a product of external influences? What are my sources of validation? Is it me myself, consciously considered, or is it me as a reflection of what's around? If my surroundings are the scope of my vision, if my views mirror those of my Facebook page, it can have profound implications. 'Me' risks being a creation of others.

Reality starts with you, Kate. When you step out into the world to carve your own paths, you will be a relatively free agent; the world will literally be your oyster, and yet, at that point, you will know little of the world and there will be many influences that, like magnets, will be pulling you in certain directions. Your past and your present to start with. For better or worse, you've taken on a mixture of learnings, opinions and principles from your mother and me, from your family and friends, from school, from your phone, and what you know now is largely a reflection of those and the domain you currently exist in. This is your world at present; you had little choice in it so I hope that it has largely been a positive influence for you!

But to start to create your own identity, you need to understand those influences and how they've influenced you. Unpicking and then rebuilding in your own way is how you start to develop your self-understanding. If you seek reality and truth in life, then you must also have an honest dialogue with yourself. To do this you need to challenge – and keep challenging – assumptions and preconceptions.

Knowing yourself is not a static picture; it is a journey, an exploration of your potential. But how do you know what you're capable of? You don't know what you don't know, so you won't know whether you can do something new or not or whether you will like it or not, unless you try. And this is the crux of seeking to make the most out of your life. It is not just a mindset of exploring truths but a process of enquiry, learning and improvement and it is, or should be, never-ending.

Your scope and vision are for you to define. The central word in this is 'you' and if you consciously try, you can spend your whole life discovering new things about yourself and what you're capable of. What a journey that can be.

I hope with all my heart you travel it far.

Dad xx

3. Values

Bangkok
August 1985

'Him!' The police officer was pointing at my buddy, Graham; several policemen immediately pushed his face down on the bonnet of a car and pulled his arms behind to handcuff him.

It was bewildering.

We had just been having a night out in Bangkok with a couple of people we had met at the hostel. It was the early hours of the morning; we'd been for a meal. The Swiss guy had refused to pay for his water as it was too expensive, he said. The rest of us had paid up. We'd then gone outside to discuss what to do next. The Aussie had pulled out a joint and thrown it away; we were about to move on to a bar, when four police cars suddenly pulled up around us.

Sirens and flashing lights illuminated the scene as crowds started to develop on the sidelines. And we were in the centre of the set, surrounded by agitated policemen, gesticulating and shouting.

'No understand.' All I could think to do was play the dumb tourist. Initially there was just confusion and more agitation; but then a policeman picked up an old filter butt from the street and started pointing at it. 'Drugs' was the only word I caught, but that was enough. The movie was getting real.

The boss clearly had had enough. He pointed to Graham. Slow motion suddenly went into fast forward. In no time he was in the back of a police car, fading into the Bangkok night. The Swiss and Aussie disappeared into the crowds.

I tried calling local police stations; of the ones I could communicate with, they knew nothing. It was four in the morning as I lay staring at the fan in our hostel room going round and round, just like my head and my stomach. Visions of the film *Midnight Express* flashed through my mind; had Graham been thrown into a prison like that? The night and solitude are no friends of the rational.

I wrestled my brain to think. 'Call the Embassy' was the best I could come up with. They must have seen this kind of thing before. I phoned at one minute after nine. They had.

'There's a prison specifically for foreigners, he's most likely there. But come back to us if he isn't,' said the voice down the line. He didn't sound judgemental and that helped. I wrote down the address and rushed out of the door, hailing the first tuk-tuk, not even asking the price.

I was directed to a small man hunched over a large desk stacked with files. He didn't look up at me. At the umpteenth attempt to get a dialogue going, I produced Graham's passport. The man paused, studied me through his round spectacles and then looked over at a list. 'Yes, he's here.' Encouraged, I produced our flight tickets and explained we were leaving the country in a week's time and wanted to go to Chiang Mai.

Then just like that, he said he would release him.

I sagged in the chair and closed my eyes.

After I don't know how long, Graham appeared through a side door, seemingly in better shape than me. 'I keep your passport,' the man said, waving it at Graham. 'You come back in a week.'

Seven days later, we came back on the overnight bus from Chiang Mai, leaving us a day in Bangkok before our flights. Graham headed straight off to the prison, agreeing to meet for a beer late afternoon.

Five came, then six, then seven, and nothing. Where was he? Had he been mugged? Was he at the prison? Why would he be? – they had said he could pick up his passport and go. Our flights were due out the next day at midday; they were non-changeable, non-refundable, non-everything. It was impossible to sleep; I packed both our bags but did not have a clue how the next day would unfold. All I could do was go back to the prison and take it from there. The idea that I might be faced with a decision to leave Graham in Bangkok flashed into my mind. No, you're here till this is resolved, I said to myself. The idea of writing off those flights hurt, but more still did the thought that I might be calling our respective parents to explain the situation and ask for help. Our small hostel room felt like a lonely prison cell, except I had a bed. What was Graham sleeping on tonight?

I was the first person through the doors of the prison the next day and was ushered in front of the same man as before. He was surveying his piles of papers. I tried again to engage; he didn't even look up. After twenty minutes, my frustration slammed my fist into the table; I felt helpless and out of control. He raised his eyebrows. Silence. I breathed in. He finally spoke.

'He is here,' he said, looking pointedly at me.

'How do I get him out?' I asked. He quoted a number in baht that I didn't even bother to convert into pounds; I went to my money belt to see if I had enough and counted out the notes in front of him.

'You'll let him go then?'

'We will bring him to the airport to meet you.'

'I'd like to see him, please.'

He looked twice at me, but then gestured to someone to his right. I followed. We went outside and there was a large rectangular single-storey building with iron bars in small windows, like a dusty Mexican jail from a wild west movie.

After muffled shouts inside, the guard pulled Graham out.

'You're OK?' I asked.

He nodded, with that familiar grin on his face. I told him that I had paid for his release and he'd be brought to the airport. He told me there were people he had met in there who'd been in for months, whose families didn't even know they were there. He had had two bowls of rice since I had seen him last. Time was not on our side to chat though.

'See you later,' I said, somewhat weakly, as I turned to head back to get our bags, not knowing really what was going to happen next, but knowing all I could do was get to the airport and wait and hope.

An hour before departure, my nerves in shreds, Graham was led in handcuffs by a policeman in plain clothes to the check-in desk. Graham pulled out his passport from his front pocket and handed it over the counter with his two hands still bound together.

'This is my friend I was telling you about. Here's his bag,' I stuttered. The reservations lady didn't say much.

The cuffs didn't come off till we were in the departure area. Stares were all around as Graham was seated in front of the gate, but I was beyond caring. It looked like the nightmare was over; the world could go to hell right now.

'How did you get in this mess?' the cop asked.

We told him the story.

He shook his head in a knowing, fatherly way. 'It was the lady in the restaurant; she must have known someone in the police,' he said. 'It wasn't good to cross her.'

Graham and I had paid her in full but we'd become collateral damage.

'And there are ways to make these things go away too,' he said.

I haven't paid a bribe still to anyone to this day; but fortunately, I haven't had to fish anyone from a Bangkok prison since…

***

'I have learned that as long as I hold fast to my beliefs and values – and follow my own moral compass – then the only expectations I need to live up to are my own.'

Michelle Obama

Kate,

Your values will define how you journey through your life, and with whom.

You will develop, you will learn, you will get wiser; your attitudes will change about those around you, about yourself, about life itself. But your values should be true and they should be unwavering. We live inside our consciousness, so while what we do can turn out to be wrong but can often be rectified, how we do it lives with us; if we have broken our word or followed others' opinions or actions against our values, these gnaw at us; they eat into our self-worth.

For me, the foundations of a value system are based around two core principles – respect and integrity.

<u>Respect</u>
All people, all things, deserve respect, at least to begin with, at least until they demonstrate that they don't deserve it. What does this mean?

Not assuming that you're better than others, or you're right and they're wrong – essentially trying to avoid preconceptions and prejudices, which we all have to a greater or lesser extent, however much we think we don't, and treating people 'as you would want to be treated'. It means listening with consideration not deafness. Whether it's with people or with nature, being respectful also means humility and politeness.

While manners are viewed increasingly as a cultural artefact, they are in fact an important sign of respect in our ever more self-absorbed lifestyles. They are important symbols between two people of the ongoing recognition and respect held between them. When they are not present, it is an outward sign of taking the other for granted or symbols of a dysfunctional relationship. Maybe you don't need a guy to open the door for you, but basic human manners should never be forgotten.

Humility develops with an understanding of what you know and, more significantly, a realisation of what you don't know in this world. It is an attribute of the enquiring spirit. It comes from knowing that values are not driven by wealth and education and that appearances are often deceptive. It comes from knowing that we all make mistakes, that random things can happen through life that can knock us down and that we often do not know the background to others' situations, thus risking making false assumptions about others' motives. While arrogance lies in those of small vision and poor self-awareness, humility understands that we can improve and that we are never the finished article. It makes us appreciate that others have an opinion and makes us take the time to listen – however sure we are of our argument.

I read recently a story of someone enrolled in an evening management course; he always sat in the same chair, as most of us do, always next to the same man. But this guy would always have one of his bags on this chap's chair and they would follow the same ritual each time, of the Arab greeting him warmly and lifting his bag off the chair. The man was annoyed at this – why couldn't he just keep his bags to himself? – but he said nothing.

Till the day he got delayed outside the classroom taking a call and he saw someone come in and try to sit at 'his' chair, and he saw the Arab telling him that he was keeping it for his friend. He then realised that, all along, the guy had been looking out for him. He went in and shook his hand and took him out to lunch. From strangers, they became friends. But it could easily not have happened; we all have preconceptions that can wrongly colour our views and opinions.

Humility does not mean, though, being a 'shrinking violet' or weak in personality; indeed, it is the opposite. Those confident in themselves, their environment and their views do not generally feel the need to shout about them, their successes or to try to demean others. It is the strength of mind to be able to admit you're wrong and apologise but also to recognise disrespect in others and be able to walk away from it.

Integrity

Integrity is about you and how you deal with the outside world. To me, it has two parts: being true to others and being true to yourself; being true is about being consistent. If there is no consistency in the application of your principles then, internally, you have no base or foundation to improve upon and, externally, you have no basis for developing and maintaining positive relationships.

Being true to others means keeping to your word; you do what you say you're going to do. It is the basis for any valuable relationship, whether personal or business, and while it may not be the only means to judge the strength of a relationship by, it is the means to judge weak ones.

Actions may define people and ultimately it is only by doing that we achieve anything, but words are how we interact (and transact) as humans. Integrity is about these interactions.

I have only known a few people in my life whom I can say really operated by the dictum 'my word is my bond'. One of them was someone I worked for, and then later with. Mike left school at sixteen with few qualifications but soon started his own business; he was hard, stubborn to the point of pig-headedness and often rude. But he had two features, apart from his intellect, that were core to his success: he would work harder than anyone else and he would always do what he said. His handshake was better than any legal agreement. And by this, he commanded incredible loyalty from his staff, his customers and his suppliers and over the course of his life sold several businesses very successfully. He kept his word, I think, because he felt it was the right thing to do; but he also was able to look over short-term costs or pain for the longer term.

So it is with you; if you take what you say seriously and follow through on actions you've committed to or honour words you've shaken hands on, you will build the trust and loyalty of others.

Sometimes this is far from easy and there will be temptations and sometimes gains to be had by not doing so. In such situations, it is important to remember that a good reputation is hard won but easily lost and a bad one easily gained, and often hard to lose.

Being true to yourself is about being consistent with who you are and your principles and it is about translating these into (words and) actions in your dealings with others. Throughout your journey through life you will be confronted by people and situations that are new to you and you will be open to influence from them, which can of course be either good or bad. It is what influences you choose and to what extent they influence you that is important. This is where knowing yourself and your values comes in; if you do not live true to them, you will live like a candle in the wind, or take your reference points reactively from others.

Values are what you use to deal with everything life throws at you. They are the constants, the anchors and references in your life. Values define how you act each day. They should define who your friends are and how you interact with people at all levels, from strangers to family. They are what help you outside a Bangkok prison.

Setting your own moral compass, as Michelle Obama says, is the easy part; living it is what counts. Above all, value your word; it will define much of your journey and with whom you journey.

Travel well!
Dad xx

4. Small Steps

Nepal: Annapurna base camp trek
October 1992

'You're going to have to take off the whole sole?' I looked at the boot and its flapping sole and saw my base camp dreams slipping between my fingers.

I turned to the phlegmatic, wrinkled face of the man sitting on a small stool in front of me, knees into his chest, barefoot. He didn't look like a cobbler; he certainly wasn't busy. But what other option did I have?

My left Timberland boot had come apart a few miles further back. The porters had said there was a village nearby where there should be some shoes to buy at a shop. I wondered what on earth they could be like but with little other apparent choice to hand I wrapped string around my sorry boot and soldiered on. Anger at Timberland and resignation at my predicament filled my head as we snaked the trail up and down hillsides; even the rich, layered paddy fields, the smiling toothless old ladies looking up from their work, and the running, waving kids shouting 'namaste' failed to change my mood.

The village was a slightly larger version of many we had passed through; in the middle was a lodge-cum-restaurant-cum, as it turned out, shop. There were a few packets of biscuits and bottles of Coke in a glass cabinet.

An old lady, dressed in bright traditional Nepali clothing, stood proudly behind.

'Namaste,' she greeted us, with a huge warm smile.

'Namaste,' I nodded, and desperate to know whether she could ease my situation, 'do you have any shoes?' I asked, half expecting her to start laughing.

Instead, after exchanging a few words in Nepali with one of our porters, she disappeared into a back room and returned a few minutes later with a plastic bag from which she proudly pulled some blue and pink plastic sandals.

The largest pair I could find was size four. Nepali shoes. I sat disconsolately on a step, abandoning the prospect of wandering at the feet of those mountain gods above us, and turning instead to how I would even get down from there.

The lady, her round, wrinkled face turning from smile to concern as she studied me, saw my boot and immediately started gesturing me to follow her outside. She led me to a small hut close by. 'He fix' was all I got from her before she turned back to the lodge.

So there I was, my dream in this man's hands and needle. 'How long will it take?' I asked weakly. 'My friends want to leave soon.'

'Half hour,' was the reply.

I was getting used to time management in Nepal but this was ridiculous. I told him to proceed and slopped back to the lodge to order a beer to take the edge off my circumstance. I looked at David* and James.

'I think you guys may be going up on your own,' I told them as I slumped down on a plastic chair. They ordered a beer too. We talked awkwardly; they knew how much I had wanted to do this.

The cobbler turned up forty minutes later.

He held out a perfectly stitched boot as if it were the most routine thing. I grabbed it and tried it on. It was tight but perfect. Stronger, I was sure, than before. I wanted to kiss the man. I handed him treble

---

* There are two Davids in various stories of my life: David Pitblado, with whom I climbed on Aconcagua, and David Walker, with whom I went to Alaska and Nepal, both the closest of friends. This is David Walker.

what he asked and beamed at everyone. Even the old lady gave a little clap as I marched triumphantly around her courtyard.

Everything was so sweet going up from there; a man reprieved, I missed nothing. The hiking itself became a treasure, the path to ourselves but for intermittent villagers with large baskets on their backs, balanced on ropes from their heads. They moved like goats over the rocks and angles. Sometimes with headphones on, I would get into a trance-like rhythm, subsumed into the grandeur of the visions in front. Sometimes I would stop to watch kids playing with whatever they could find on the ground or running around barefoot chasing a disgruntled chicken while mothers and grandmothers worked tirelessly in the fields, their bright colours illuminating the deep greens and radiating in the sunshine. But always a look up and a smile in response to my greeting. The humility of these people touched me deeply; it seemed part of their closeness to their surrounds and it warmed me.

As we got higher, the hillside paths opened up into a wider plain; we were getting closer to Herzog's mountain and its sisters and the 'Fishtail' peak, Machapuchare, a sacred jagged beauty whose peak is untouched by man.

My first views of any of the Himalayan giants. The route is called the Sanctuary trek because it is or was held to be a sacred place by the local Gurung people; it feels like a sanctuary, too, with its narrow entrance between two huge peaks, which then opens up to flat terrain encircled on all sides by slopes that rise to the skies. We couldn't see much as we entered base camp, as the sun was going down behind the mountains and the cold was drifting down quickly. We settled by the hut's fire with blankets; our outside bunks and flimsy sleeping bags presaged an uncomfortable night, but the humour was high. We were here.

The next morning, the cold forced us all up early. Wearing every layer I could find, I went out to see what we'd travelled this long path for. Would it match the quiet magnificence of the books I had read? The sky was an icy blue; yet, even at over 4,000 metres, I had to crane my neck to take it all in. Nothing could have prepared me for the power and magnificence of these giants in real life. I looked down at my boot and kissed that cobbler again.

So began my love affair with Nepal.

***

'A thousand-mile journey begins with a single step.'

Lao Tzu, *Tao Te Ching*

'The secret of getting ahead is getting started. The secret of getting started is breaking complex overwhelming tasks into small manageable tasks, and then starting with the first one.'

Attributed to Mark Twain

Kate,

That long path that snakes up the Annapurna valley goes on and on; sometimes it disappears from view and reconnects further up. You see dots of people in the distance, and then a few minutes later they are next to you. It is amazing the distance you can cover, as long as you have working boots. This is the trick of the eye and the challenge of the unfamiliar on the mind.

Every endeavour, however big or small, is a series of tasks, every journey a series of steps. And it is usually that first step that is the hardest. It is natural in everyday life for us to put off the more difficult in favour of the more familiar, or the more important for the more pressing. In our busy lives, there are always seemingly valid reasons why we can't do x or y, particularly if it is a seemingly big endeavour.

Joe Simpson, in his epic *Touching the Void*, having survived two falls and crawled out of a crevasse, had the seemingly impossible task of then getting back to base camp across a long, disjointed ice field. He had a badly broken leg and frozen fingers but was also emaciated and completely dehydrated. He knew too that he had to get back quickly to not miss his departing colleagues, who thought him dead.

'Twelve noon was the deadline, and I intended to break those hours into short stages, each one carefully timed. I searched ahead for the first landmark – a tall pillar of red rock that stood out clearly over the sea of boulders. Half an hour to reach it, and then I would look for another.'

He would never have made it back to camp in the state he was in if he hadn't broken the journey down into small milestones, like ten steps or a small landmark before the next break. This is the same for someone writing a book, starting a business or tackling a phobia.

Viewed as one amorphous endeavour, it is easy to be put off or to put off decision-making or action. Simpson had to do it to survive; it is much harder to motivate oneself when there is no compelling need.

Yet to learn a language or a musical instrument, you start with one word or one note, to sail an ocean you start in a dinghy, to run a marathon you start with a jog round the block.

If you need support, try to do it with others; if you want to keep yourself from giving up quietly, tell others of your goals; if you are unsure of the steps, involve a guide's help. If a step looks too big a leap, break it in half.

Usually, once you've taken the first step, you won't believe what all the fuss was about and why you hadn't done it before. This is the nature of things; if you could look at yourself from outside, you would more often than not be pushing yourself to have a go.

The great thing is that a small step is all that is required to get going and this is possible for everyone. And from setting small goals and achieving them can come the next ones, potentially bigger, maybe different. It is amazing what can be achieved by keeping your head down on a journey that looks too far at the start, and in a few hours, looking back at the distance you have come.

Dad xx

5. Wise Decision

Aconcagua – two tales of a mountain
25 December 1998

'*Don't turn around!*' The voice in my ear was getting fainter, as the sun and solitude beat up my spirit. The long couloir was reverberating with late-morning sun. Heat pressed in on all sides, shrinking my mind. My throat screamed for water, my body for respite from its exhaustion; sweat was glue on my skin. The rest of my party had turned around. I had no one to talk to. I really wanted to get to the top… but could I make it?

Another voice in my head chirped up…

***

My first attempt to climb Aconcagua was in 1998. I had at least done a few 6,000-metre mountains before, so maybe I had a right to be there, but my three friends were not only lacking in climbing experience, they were in varying degrees of physical fitness too. David (Pitblado) was a super-fit Canadian, tough as nails, but he'd previously got altitude sickness on a 5,000-metre pass in Nepal. Rick, a languid Brit, was a rugby player and said he'd trained for this. Finally, Jason, a huge Anglo-American, larger than life, needed to lose a few kilos but I knew he was a determined character.

Who knows – maybe it'd work. We had hired a US guide, Scott, who claimed many summits of Aconcagua and said he could get us up. He should know his stuff and look after us.

Summit day

25 December

It was a cold night and difficult to sleep but it was still a shock to be woken at 4.30 in the pitch black… We started walking at 5.30 when there were glimmers of light appearing. After an hour, Rick stopped everyone and said he was turning back. He was tired and was sure he couldn't make it. It was a shock so early… We were all pretty quiet, with our own battles, I guess…

We completed the long traverse to the Canaleta; everyone seemed to be holding up OK and Scott said we were making good progress. It was getting hot…

Dave was starting to show signs of deterioration. He kept falling back. Jason seemed to be holding up well, though also weak. With only one guide, group splitting was potentially a problem. We stopped again for Dave. Scott this time ordered him to the sidelines… 'Promise me you won't move from here.' I was taken aback by how quickly this had all happened – the scary thing about altitude, I guess. Things happen quickly but you also react more slowly…

Scott told me and Jason to carry on – he would catch up. I started on up in my own world. The next thing I know is Scott shouting up at me saying he and Jason are taking Dave down because he has the beginnings of cerebral oedema. The words are shocking enough whether you know what they mean or not. He told me to do the summit myself.

'How long before I should turn back?' I asked.

'12.30,' he replied. An hour and a half.

I stumbled up but I felt weak and had lost my momentum. Should I go up or down? I tried to rationalise, knowing my thinking wasn't straight. I didn't like being left alone on the mountain even though there were other groups… what if something happened to me? Scott had told stories of guys who had got to the top through their own guts but could hardly walk afterwards. What if that happened to me? I had a voice on each shoulder fighting the other. Push on. Turn back.

I wasn't feeling strong. My Montane kit was draining energy from me with every drop of sweat [I was wearing a one-layer top and bottom so I couldn't de-layer – big mistake in hindsight]. Time was getting on. One hour left but I wanted to do it. I pushed on further then stopped again. Loneliness fed my uncertainty.

It wasn't worth it, I decided. Get down safe. So I started down. But it kept gnawing at me.

It was just as hard, my crampons ripping my trousers as I stumbled. I took my time but was mentally drained. Now that I had decided to turn around, now that the prize was gone, the adrenalin went, to be replaced by tiredness.

What was up with David? I had to carry on. Then I came across Scott coming back up. He had left David and Jason feeling a bit better and had come back up to help me. If I had known, I would have waited…

*Scott went ahead… I stumbled into camp at 2.30ish. The talk was whether to decamp and take David down further. I was too tired to move then. If David needed to go down, Scott would have to take him. He decided to wait and see. At six we got a knock on the tent; Dave wanted to go down and Scott wanted us to go as a group. We'd have to pack up everything. ****!*

Reserves of energy, which I never knew I had but which proved I had more for the mountain with rest, pulled me together. We all packed the biggest loads we'd ever had – David couldn't carry, obviously. We arrived at the next camp, 1,500 feet below, as the sun was setting at around 9, the big face of Aconcagua looming large above us now, part of our route visible on its side, the top untamed by any of us, a dream gone by…

David sent me a framed picture of the mountain afterwards, with these words: *'Thank you for willing this unforgettable challenge into existence. It will remain a life highlight forever.'*

If I knew then what I know now, I would have done several things differently and pushed back on Scott more. He got a number of things wrong. I had it in my head that we should always follow the guide. But sometimes you still need to think for yourself and ask why and what are the options, and challenge calls.

***

Aconcagua Part 2
Mendoza
27 December 2008
Met Louis and we went out for beers and a steak. It was good to catch up, hear about his experiences on Cho Oyo and discuss Everest [which we were booked to do the next spring]. For both of us the shadow of Everest is ever present at the moment, subconsciously and consciously, whether it is organising gear, training, trying to avoid sickness or put on some spare weight (in my case).

We met Eli later; she was once again our trip organiser and fellow climber. It would be the three of us trying to go up as quickly and leanly as possible, but sensibly. There's a danger we take Aconcagua too lightly.

Summit day
9 January
The alarm went at 4.30 a.m. We'd all got some sleep but it had been cold; however, the sky was clear and the winds moderate. We were a go. After melting ice, hydrating, forcing down hot oats for breakfast and some faffing, we didn't get going till 7.30 so we weren't the first on the summit push by any means...

On the way we had to stop for a group of rescuers with a 'blood wagon', in this case a half cut out plastic barrel into which the patient was tied and wrapped up in blankets. He was alive but looked frostbitten, and at regular intervals the rescuers would shout at him to stay awake. We later found out that he was part of a small Italian team of which a female climber and an Argentinian guide had died the previous night. They had summited late and then taken a wrong turn in the white-out... Tragic, but why were they summiting so late in the day?

We carried on and caught up with other groups... One guy from the Patagonicas group was being practically pushed up – I said to Louis as we took a break that he should have been turned around long before, thinking of Pit's situation all those years ago... Fortunately, the Patagonicas guide, Jacob, did turn him around and one or two others. At a stop, I mentioned to

*Eli that we should try to get ahead of these groups so the three of us headed
out. Eli stopped to fix something; Louis and I carried on, me taking the lead.
I felt strong, though it was tough going and we were breathing heavily... I
arrived at the summit at about 2.30, Louis about ten minutes after, Eli ten
after him.*

Louis and I, though, were keen to get going back down...

*The descent was around 3 hours – in total we'd been going for 10 hours
and we were glad to see our tent and get the hot drinks going. As we rested,
Eli came back having spoken again on the radio to Jacob – apparently that
sick chap on the summit had died! And later we heard that another guy
hadn't made it... Four dead while we were on the mountain! Shocking on
any mountain, but on Aconcagua?*

*The numbers climbing here have increased exponentially, as have the
guiding companies promising success. They all make it sound like they
can get you to the top whoever you are... Aconcagua can be a very tough
mountain and its weather, as we had experienced, can change in an instant.
You have to respect the mountain and be well prepared.*

11 January

We were finally in a jeep after a 20-mile hike out, heading back to
Mendoza. The sky ahead was a glorious mixture of dark rumbling
clouds and orange sunset. The heavens opened and we were suddenly
crawling along at 10 mph in over a foot of flash-flood rains. 'The
Scientist' by Coldplay came on the radio... *'Nobody said it was easy...'*
Every time I hear that song and those words, I smile; memories of that
moment and the preceding few days come back, the mixture of
satisfaction and tiredness, though tinged by some shock at the tragedies
we'd been witnesses to.

Compared to ten years previously, the mountain this time had had
far fewer anxieties and unknowns; I had come a long way in that time.
It was hard but we felt in control of our position and able to react to
events as they occurred. The deaths, though, were a reminder of the

realities up high, and a reminder to treat Everest with the respect it deserved, as if that was needed.

***

'The possession of wisdom shows itself in reliable, sound, reasonable, in a word, good judgment. In good judgment, a person brings his knowledge to bear on his actions. To understand wisdom, we have to understand its connection with knowledge, action, and judgment.'

John Kekes, 'Wisdom', *American Philosophical Quarterly*, 20/3, 1983

'… it is evident that it is impossible to be practically wise without being good.'

Aristotle, *Nicomachean Ethics*, 1144a, VI.12

Dear Kate,

How do you make decisions? Logic, gut feel, emotions? Sometimes one and not the other, sometimes a bit of everything? Which wins through?

That decision to turn around on Aconcagua was tough; I had a voice in one ear telling me not to be a wimp and carry on, and another trying to think rationally, but all the time, nagged by solitude and nerves. I think I made the right call in the end but the 'what ifs' are still there.

One of the greatest mountaineering books is *Annapurna* by Maurice Herzog. The first time I read it on a climb in Ecuador, its brave simplicity brought me to tears in my tent. I thought they were all heroes. As I have learnt more through my climbing, I've come to question that. On the summit push with his companion Louis Lachenal, Herzog recounts:

> '*The going was incredibly exhausting, and every step was a struggle of mind over matter. …*

Lachenal continued to complain of his feet.

> *"I can't feel anything." … I began to be seriously worried. … Nor was Lachenal under any illusions. "We're in danger of having frozen feet. Do you think it's worth it?"'*

Further up, he stops Herzog.

'Suddenly, Lachenal grabbed me. "If I go back, what will you do?"

A whole sequence of pictures flashed through my head. … Must we give up? No, that would be impossible. I had made up my mind irrevocably. Today we were consecrating an ideal, and no sacrifice was too great. My voice rang out clearly; "I should go on by myself."

If he wished to go down it was not for me to stop him. He must make his own choice freely.

"Then I'll follow you."'

Whatever Herzog says, Lachenal really had little option at that point; he had to go with Herzog. They succeeded in being the first people to summit an 8,000-metre mountain, an incredible achievement without oxygen, but their descent had terrible consequences; they lost almost all of their fingers and toes. Lachenal never came to terms with his disabilities after; he was like an 'eagle with clipped wings' according to one of their team mates, and died in a skiing accident five years later. Herzog's book is heroic and hugely impactful, but he chooses to focus little on the dark sides of the decision he took that day.

Thinking at nearly 8,000 metres is not the easiest. Herzog felt the weight of France, and history, bearing on him; but he also had a team to consider. But he didn't think. He had already made up his mind – *no sacrifice was too great*. Maybe that would be OK if it was just him, but he knew Lachenal couldn't really leave him.

On my first trip to Aconcagua, I decided to turn round; I will never know if I could have made it up. On the second, we encountered the deaths of four people who had made different decisions in the storms of that trip. Herzog and Lachenal survived their mountain, just, but with lifelong consequences.

Making good decisions is tough; we are only human after all!

But making bad decisions is quite easy – or at least increasing our chances of a bad decision. 'I went with my feelings', 'I went with my heart' are good starting points.

Such decisions are emotional, can be a cop-out or just plain lazy; and they are often wrong. No thinking has been involved, presumably no discussion – because that would involve justifying a position – and no consideration of options or alternatives. I may as well throw a dart at the board, blindfolded.

What is the alternative?

Thinking.

There are certain decisions that can be largely, if not solely, based on logic or calculation. A business investment would be a prime example but there are many in everyday life. If it is a practical issue, then this might be the 'most healthy' or 'quickest route' or whatever is the aim of the decision-making process.

But many decisions are not purely calculations, even in business. In a perfect world, we'd have all the information to hand, all the options and all the time to consider the best decision. But of course, life isn't like that. We often need to make 'the best decision we can with the information available'. What should we do? How do we learn to make better, wiser decisions?

As Aristotle says, it is impossible to be wise without being good. One cannot make any decision without reference to one's values. They come to the fore the more feelings are involved. Or they should!

When you come to consider your partner in life, for instance, values not passions are your best decision support. You may have two gremlins whispering in your ears, like I did on Aconcagua, but you need to hear both out, and think through your decision. Even in love, deciding just 'with your heart' is a risky path.

Kekes said wisdom shows itself in good judgement and '*In good judgment, a person brings his knowledge to bear on his actions*'. Knowledge is clearly important in making a decision, especially in the more logical ones. But judgement is so much more than just knowledge-based.

When there's imperfect information or insufficient time, two counter-playing factors often get involved in our decision-making: our emotions and our instinct. If emotions prevail, it may not only be a bad decision but it is also likely to elicit an emotional response back. How do all fights start?

Instinct is based on our subconscious and our conscious self. The subconscious is all the opinions, rituals and ideas we have absorbed from our past and our surrounds. The conscious is all that we've experienced and processed in life ourselves. It is all we have gained from our pool of experiences.

If my instinct is based on a limited perspective, my decision-making will reflect that. I will see few options and most will be based on the habits and views of who and what I have grown up with or see around me. If I am not consciously building up my own experiences and learnings, then 'the way it has always been done' will be what prevails. That can, of course, be fine. But it is not trying to make wiser decisions.

The wider your experiences, the larger the pool you have to draw on when making decisions; the more you've reflected on your influences, the less preconceived will be your viewpoint; the more willing to explore and try, the more you'll search for options, the apparent and the hidden. Wiser judgement is based on an open and inquisitive mind that does not settle just for what it is told.

I knew so much more by my second attempt on Aconcagua; I was more informed and my instincts were better. We made good decisions on that mountain, even when circumstances changed and the storm came in.

Herzog chose to ignore his instincts and those of his partner. It would have cost them their lives but for others risking theirs to save them. Good knowledge, instinct and values are nothing without conscious deliberation – even at 8,000 metres. This creates a virtuous circle, because it is how you grow and how you learn to make better decisions the next time.

Wisdom goes beyond knowledge and judgement to involve perspective and understanding in a more holistic way. It has a practical angle; it brings an ability to contextualise, to relate to life as widely as possible. Hence the term 'worldly wise', perhaps. It involves an understanding of life and an empathy for others. Understanding of life brings in your experiences and your tolerances for the uncertainties and ups and downs in life and empathy brings in how you interact and relate to others.

When I play chess, which is very infrequently, I make a lot of mistakes; I probably only evaluate a tiny fraction of the potential moves available to me and I often pay for it. Garry Kasparov would see many times my number of options, partly because he's a lot smarter than me and partly because he has been playing and studying chess all his life; he has seen countless moves before and has many pre-set moves or responses already in his head. He sees patterns and strategies where I see a rook in trouble.

Like Kasparov, the more you consciously experience life, the more 'expert' you become in it, the wiser will be your judgement and the more enlightened your understanding of life and your empathy. You will get better at reading situations and people. This process never stops, if you keep learning from each move like Kasparov.

You'll make bad decisions in life, and wrong ones. You can do much to lessen them by honest reflection and honest reaction. You should never feel too proud to apologise. But you should also never shirk from making decisions; they are integral to making the most out of life and this is why trying to get a bit wiser each day is so important.

Good luck!

Dad xx

6. Don't Settle
When You Settle

Pamplona
July 1999

The smell hits me. I don't have time to think that it's true – you really can smell fear – till later. It's all happening so quickly; the air pulses with static and sweat. I look back at a sea of red and white pouring up the cobbled street, the early morning heat whitening the sprinting, squinting faces, the shouting getting louder… and the screaming.

***

The San Fermin festival is seven days of twenty-four-hour partying, a whole town centre shut off for the purpose, bars open in every nook and cranny, huge outdoor eating and drinking areas, daytime street processions, banging drums, and hordes and hordes of revelling, happy people. I have been to Pamplona six times and not seen any trouble; this is despite heaving crowds in the bars and streets, trying to get to the next event or the next *cerveza*. People smile, apologise, put their arms around each other. The homogeneity of costume helps, white head to foot but for a red sash and neckerchief. It levels and unites; when drinks are spilt, it is part of the dues.

My most regular companions were Katherine, Jason, Holly and

Sally, though each time there'd be normally six to eight of us. Our fading sashes, weathered by previous visits, were symbols of honour and folklore, washed and tucked away in drawers, brought out annually for the ritual. Off the plane, walking to our hotel in the town centre, pale-faced, the heat reflecting off the cobbles, the air permeated with stale alcohol, through the bemused morning faces of the night before, we felt like outsiders walking through a stage show. But as the anticipation built, we'd recount tales and point out landmarks to 'virgins' to the festival. We'd quickly change, the San Fermin wardrobe immediately making us feel like we'd arrived, that we were now ready to take part, the excitement rising as we stepped out into the sun for that first afternoon lunch. We would head to the big outdoor eating area, a little out from the centre; it was our usual spot. It was also our way of trying to adjust to the rhythm of San Fermin.

For most, the festivities work around the bull run; this means staying up all night to be ready to participate or to watch as the bulls are released at eight each morning. Unless you're planning to go to bed and get up early (hardly the point of San Fermin), this means altering your body clock completely. The way we learnt to tackle this was to go to bed after the run and wake for a mid-afternoon lunch, then wander the town a bit perhaps, and then back to the hotel for another sleep early evening.

Forcing a wake-up at around eleven at night was totally counter to the body's natural inclination but once we went out into the crowds, the buzz immediately banished the lethargy of sleep and lifted the spirits. It was important to schedule dinner at around three o'clock, to get some sitting time and respite, before the push through to sunlight. If you were running the bulls, coffee and water would replace alcohol at about six in the morning. It was a tough schedule but you could work it for a few days.

***

43

8 July 1999

We arrived at the marquees; it felt like we were just picking up from the previous year. Huge paella pans bubbled away and whole chickens darkened on rotisseries, filling our nostrils with anticipation. We sat down at long tables with bottles of chilled rosé and started to recount stories of previous trips. There was nothing but laughter at idiocies or comical mishaps or just the pure fun had. But there would always be the question of who was running the bulls and when.

'What should I do? Talk me through it. Should I go for it tonight?' David was full of questions; it was his first visit to the festival. For most first-timers, it is one of those horrible 'I really can't not do this now I'm here, but I'd rather get it over very quickly' things.

After lunch, we headed to the square in front of the town hall. 'This is where it starts,' I said. 'Everyone crowds in here before ten to eight in the morning.'

'At eight,' Jason went on, 'the gun goes. That's the signal for the start.'

'So you are allowed to go from here when the gun goes,' Katherine said. We followed the cobbled road up and round a ninety-degree bend to a long straight street leading up to the bullring. 'All these shops and bars are shut up,' she carried on, pointing to all the doors along the way, 'so people will try to take cover in the doorways but there aren't too many spots so it's a risky strategy!'

We halted halfway up the street. 'The officials stop everyone around here,' I said, looking at David, 'and you wait till a second gun goes. That's when the bulls are released. If a third gun goes soon after, that means the bulls are not together. So they are more disorientated and can cause more trouble.'

'Does that change tactics?' David asked.

'Well, there aren't too many places to go!' Katherine said, looking around. 'If you want to, you can go all the way to the bullring without seeing the bulls. But that's not running the bulls – and the crowds in the ring really let you know about it! You've got to go into the ring *after* the bulls.' David's eyes widened, looking at the narrowness of the street and the lack of potential escape.

'The biggest issue, though, is the other people,' I said as we headed further up towards the ring. 'I could say "follow me" to you but I know it's impossible to keep an eye on each other. It's mayhem. As soon as the bulls are in range, it turns into a stampede and as people look back, they don't look forward, and that's how people fall over and how issues can happen with the bulls. Make sure you look forward more than you look back!'

We stopped in front of the stadium gates. Jason continued, 'Assuming the bulls go in front of you, the crowds are amazing – it'll be the closest you'll get to running out at Wembley. But be careful – the bulls can turn round inside. Head for the sides quickly and be ready to jump the boards in the extreme. They're quite high but it's amazing what a bit of fear can do for you!'

David was looking really worried now. 'Maybe I'll watch the first day to check it out.' I looked at Jason and Katherine. 'Are we doing it tomorrow morning?'

'Let's get it done,' Jason quickly came back. Once you're committed, the butterflies start. We headed back to the hotel to rest but the first evening it's hard. At eleven, we met in the lobby. 'Get any sleep?' I looked around; most heads shook. 'Dozed a bit,' said Katherine. And then we were out into the throng. The streets were now filled with white and red, moving sambas snaking through crowds, in and out of bars, the noise of partying filling the air.

'Where first?' We looked at each other, recalling the old haunts. 'Let's go to the bar in the corner of the square, might get a seat outside.' And so the evening started.

***

Squashed into the square just before eight, I look at David's face in front of me and then over to Jason and Katherine. There's a nervous buzz over the whole crowd; you can feel it. The smell of alcohol and sweat sits in the background but adrenalin is taking over the senses now. David's eyes are fully dilated, the conversation broken, attention easily drawn to a new sound or sight. 'What's the time?' he asks for the nth time. We are all sobering up quickly.

Jason looks at him. 'We'll go up to the halfway point together, but after that, I'll see you in the ring or if not, at the meeting point outside.' The first gun goes off. The atmosphere is still quite relaxed as we half-run up the street to the waiting point. People are chatting and laughing; maybe some of it is bravado, but at that point there's no rush. It's a beautiful crisp morning, though that is furthest from the thoughts at that moment. The second gun goes and everyone holds their breath. We look at each other. A third one doesn't come.

'We're good,' I smile. 'Good luck, enjoy it and see you at the other end.' That's the last I directly see of them. The crowd is bunching up; some have run off ahead but most are walking or jogging, waiting for the rush to start. Nerves heighten, the palms sweat; I jog on the spot, my insides churning. Looking down the street, I hear the noise escalating, then jogging turns to sprinting, smiles to anxiety. The smell of fear fills the air. They're nearly here.

It's all in slow motion. I try to time my sprint; I want to keep in front till the wider patch of road and stay out of trouble but I nearly stumble on someone ahead who changes direction. The cobbles rear up in front of me, slippery from alcohol. I just about avoid starting a pile-up behind. Suddenly, the human field is fanning out as the bulls close in. They are moving at pace, but in a pack; the leader is charging up the middle of the road. If I stay on this line, they'll go by me by a couple of metres. It's all so quick; they've nearly passed me. I start laughing as I run, a nervous laugh of exultation, and then it is into the tunnel of the bullring and I know to be wary. But the bulls run straight through and I have a brief moment to look at the cheering crowds and jump up and down with the other runners. Adrenalin flushes away; a lightness of spirit takes over, and whooping laughter. I spot David with a broad smile. 'Wow,' he shouts, 'that was the best thing ever!'

***

'The secret for harvesting from existence the greatest fruitfulness and the greatest enjoyment is – *to live dangerously*! Build your cities on the slopes of Vesuvius!'

Nietzsche, *The Gay Science*

'It is not the strongest or the most intelligent who will survive but those who can best manage change.'

Charles Darwin (paraphrased)

Dear Kate,

There are some people who live their entire lives not just on the slopes of Vesuvius but near its rim. There are others who shy from the smallest risk.

The trouble with seeking to avoid risk is that life is not linear. Change is a constant. Even if we don't want to change, others around us will change. Even if we're happy doing the same thing at work, it is likely that our work will change. Then there are the unforeseen or random events that happen on us: health issues, deaths of loved ones, being dumped by a partner – there is much to deal with in life.

Routine can feel like a sanctuary in such circumstances, and indeed it is. The challenge is when the ruts of routine become too deep to see out of. The more rote in life, the more the slightest knock or deviation can affect. We become less able to deal with the random or the new. This can create a cycle of lowering confidence in abilities and a further retreat to routine. The less we do, the less we feel capable of doing. The less we push our boundaries, the more ossified they become. It can become a self-reinforcing, shrinking zone of comfort.

A friend of mine had a big job, but it was crazy hours. We saw her infrequently and often when we did she was really tired. So she quit. She definitely needed the break personally but nothing has replaced it; she has done a few part-time things. She has kept herself 'busy'. But when I see her, I find little to discuss; I see someone who is increasingly defensive and who is in a relationship with someone who is taking her for granted. I see this decreasing circle of confidence, manifested in all aspects of her being. But she does not.

Such a life is premised on risk minimisation and change avoidance. At best, it tries to go on without too much bad happening; it seeks to avoid unhappiness rather than strive for happiness. I said elsewhere that the bigger you make your world, the bigger it will make you. Of course, the opposite is true too; the smaller you make it, the smaller it will make you. I say this only as a warning.

The frog when put into a pan of boiling water jumps to safety; the frog in a pan of cold water that is gradually heated, dies. If we constantly challenge or get challenged, we will jump from the water. But if we've been in there too long, we may have lost the confidence to even try. This can lead to reactions such as '*Is this it?*' or '*Is this the rest of my life?*', a feeling of being stuck and unable to do anything about it, if and when reflection sets in.

It's the difference between struggling for meaning and trying to maximise meaning, between not being interested in one's potential and seeking to exploit one's potential. If you keep showjumping, but only ever jump over the same fences in the same ring for the rest of your life, what would be the point of that? There would be little meaning in going round for the nth time again.

As you know, I keep that scratch map of the world you gave me open on a side table in my study. When we went through it together with a coin, rubbing out places I had been to, country by country, we said at the time how little it looked like we had scratched off. I remind myself of that regularly.

Thoreau concludes his book *Walden* with:

> '*I left the woods for as good a reason as I went there. Perhaps it seemed to me that I had several more lives to live, and could not spare any more time for that one. It is remarkable how easily and insensibly we fall into a particular route, and make a beaten track for ourselves. ... The surface of*

the earth is soft and impressible by the feet of men; and so with the paths which the mind travels. How worn and dusty, then, must be the highways of the world, how deep the ruts of tradition and conformity! I did not wish to take a cabin passage, but rather to go before the mast and on the deck of the world, for there I could best see the moonlight amid the mountains. I do not wish to go below now.'

Try to remember this as you start to settle down in life; it is a natural thing for us all to want to do. It isn't about being the best showjumper or climber but seeking to be the best you; you do that by exploring your potential throughout life. It's not about big goals or superhuman effort and it's not about settling down on Vesuvius; it's just about not settling down when you settle down.

Love always,

Dad xx

7. Friendship

Antarctica 2005

New York
May 2004

Wendy took the call in a cab in New York. David[**] had died. She didn't need to finish the call for me to know; her eyes said it all.

I had put the business trip off for a long time and then decided to risk it for a week; I'd been worried throughout that something would happen, and it had. Wendy finished the call and we looked at each other and hugged. A part of my energy flew out of that cab window into the sunshine.

***

Mount Vinson, Antarctica, summit ridge
3 December 2005
Finally, into the rocks, over a couple of tricky shelves and the summit was in sight up a ridge! I had been thinking of David earlier when the going was getting a bit tough. All of a sudden I started crying into my goggles and I cried all the way to the top. I sat down to still myself.

[**] There are two Davids in various stories of my life: David Pitblado, with whom I climbed on Aconcagua, and David Walker, with whom I went to Alaska and Nepal, both the closest of friends. This is David Pitblado.

51

I had come to Antarctica to experience the greatest wilderness left to man, but also because I could think of no better place to finish up one set of conversations with David and start a new one.

It didn't begin well.

22 November

I had landed in Punta Arenas to meet my climbing partners and neither of my bags had landed with me. Worse, Iberia didn't have a clue where they were; and worse still, for me at least, we were immediately on high alert for a take-off slot to Antarctica.

You can sometimes be waiting for a long time for the Russian Ilyushin plane to have an appropriate weather window at Patriot Hills, but we were apparently 'in luck'. While friends in the UK hounded Iberia, I tried to see what I could buy or borrow or rent.

Suddenly it all went ballistic.

Things were moving very quickly. We got the 'GO' call – everyone was being picked up in 2 hours and I still only had a fraction of the gear I needed.

Then I got a call from Katherine that Iberia had said my bags were arriving shortly. I couldn't believe it; it might all come together! I got the OK from Vern, our guide, to go to the airport myself and meet them there. I rushed to finish packing what I had and jumped into a cab.

At the tiny airport hall, I waited at the only baggage carousel. I got dizzy focusing on it… then finally one of my bags came through. The one with my South Pole gear in it; where was my climbing bag? It must come. They always come together, don't they?

It didn't come… aaarghhh!!! Maybe it was on the next flight. But then my team arrived and we were ushered through into departures. Would the other bag come in time? I was on edge till the last.

It didn't and here I am sitting at the back of the Russian carrier, buckled into its side with fuel drums and bags stacked up and lashed to the floor in front of me. Gantries hang above my head, plywood panels at my back – it is the barest of bare shells, just as I imagined it to be.

I'm here; hopefully I can borrow enough of the rest of the gear I need at Patriot Hills (crampons being the biggest concern). I try to look forward and enjoy what I have and savour the challenge ahead.

I tie David's bandana around my neck.

Patriot Hills, Antarctica

First foot on Antarctica! Wow – it feels immense. The cold hits immediately but we are lucky; there is no wind and it is bright sunshine. It is so beautiful – an endless white sea occasionally interspersed with jutting islands of rock and ice, then the next time you look, it is like a sunburnt horizon in a plane above the clouds – so pure and clean, it is mesmerising.

I think of David – he'd have loved all this… I put the Snow Patrol song 'Run' on my MP3. The words 'To think I might not see those eyes, it makes it so hard not to cry', the reason I will always associate that song with him, traverse my consciousness and I start to water behind my goggles.

We take small planes to the base camp of Mount Vinson, Antarctica's highest. At camp 2, a storm hits us.

1 December

So I do have a slightly frostbitten finger – it has gone a bit red and yellow – just going to have to be careful. Those borrowed gloves were a bit small!

Even before I got out of the tent this morning, I knew today was a no-go. The wind started slamming the tents from around 6. It was so cold last night that my watch froze inside the tent! Apparently it was -40 degrees without wind chill, so who knows what with the roaring winds – double that? It is a problem sleeping generally here; you have to stuff anything you don't want to freeze down your sleeping bag. So I've got two water bottles, pee bottle, gloves, socks and inner boots. I can hardly move in the bag and then when I do, frost from our breathing drops from the tent roof on my head. This night was especially cold – I had to stay huddled inside my bag, with just a gap out for me to breathe through… Vern [our guide] says it is the coldest he can remember.

This is the third day we've been pushed back by the storm. Frustrating but this place takes no prisoners… I hope we get the chance and if so I give it my best shot.

High camp
3 December

It looks like the good weather of yesterday has held. We're a go. I put on the recommended layers, pack my bag and clip into the rope. This is it.

We head off up a gentle thirty-degree slope. From the extreme cold of two days ago, I'm now cooking. Sweat is building; I can feel my legs weakening. I need to de-layer, but I can't. My down pants are trapped in my harness; the best I can do is unzip the legs and tuck them into the harness. It helps; I pick up energy.

The mountain is pristine white and the sky is the most pure blue. It is an unearthly place. I think of David. I see those eyes, and that wry, tight smile; memories jump, how he introduced himself to me at business school as a tree planter, our trips together in Canada and the Andes, his unfailing interest in other people, and his battle with lymphoma. Especially, I think of his last years when things were getting tough. What I am doing is nothing, I tell myself. He gently helps me on with that 'C'mon Sammy' encouragement of his. And the climb gets easier again.

Until that summit ridge, when I know I am going to make it. Then all the emotion from New York through to his funeral and celebration comes out into my goggles. I say a quiet thank you to him as I reach the summit and survey one of the most beautiful places on Earth. I sit on my own, basking in the view and my solitude till the horizons can fill me no further.

I float down the mountain the next day.

The idyllic pictures of untainted, sparkling mountains and plains with the insignificant impression of solitary climbers hauling sleds – a snail trail across a huge white glass surface shimmering in the sunlight. Magical.

Even in my tiredness, I feel truly elated. It is so real and alive. One of those moments I will treasure...
  I play Snow Patrol again and smile.

That energy that left me in New York was coming back.

***

'Of all the things that wisdom provides to help one live one's entire life in happiness, the greatest by far is the possession of friendship.'

Epicurus, *Principal Doctrines*

'Some will tell you that you are mad, and nearly all will say, "What is the use?" For we are a nation of shopkeepers ... And so you will sledge nearly alone, but those with whom you sledge will not be shopkeepers: that is worth a great deal.'

Apsley Cherry-Garrard, *The Worst Journey in the World: Antarctica, 1910–1913*

'It's not the years in your life that count. It's the life in your years.'

Attributed to Abraham Lincoln

Dear Kate,

David was a special person, to me and many others. If there is one guy who epitomised Lincoln's quote, it was him. He had no dragons to slay or strengths to prove or silences to correct. He died peacefully, not of his volition, but on his terms. Of course, when the physical presence went, I was and am left with memories, for sure, but, more significantly, I am left with his essence, what he means to me, and how he has impacted me and how I live life.

Great people change others for the better, without knowing it, just by being who they are.

One of the key fascinations in life is that from a simple, single, sometimes random interaction can come a lifelong relationship that is life-changing and life-enhancing. As Epicurus says, good relationships can be the greatest contributors to our happiness in life.

How do such relationships develop? How do you identify the valuable ones and how do you look after them?

Friendships start with shared interest and grow through shared experiences. They are tested by shared commitments. Trust builds with commitments fulfilled and as dependencies and mutual ties grow, so a relationship develops depth and roots.

Interests can change and diverge, or move at different speeds. You'll lose lovers and you'll drift from friends during life, particularly earlier in life when people can change much in their horizons and their ambitions. The ones that persist are where the shared experiences are strong but, most importantly, where values have been tested and come through.

Values set the standards of a relationship, good and bad. If I can't rely on someone, I may have fun with them, but I wouldn't ask anything serious of them. Their friendship is good for the pub – which is fine, by the way, it just needs to be understood.

Following through on our values, though, can be the hardest thing, especially if we are in love. But if we do nothing in reaction to a close one abusing them, then we are failing to be consistent. Our values lose their worth. It is worth remembering this, attributed to Eleanor Roosevelt: '*If someone betrays you once, it is his fault; if he betrays you twice, it is your fault.*'

Yet many times problems arise from misunderstandings and misinterpretations or from losing sight and perspective in relationships. Unsaid or unnoticed, paths can diverge and the mutuality underpinning them can fade. Sometimes this is just the way it is but often it is unintended. Appreciation can get blurred by the complacency of proximity. Lack of communication can turn the smallest annoyance into a structural problem.

How do you avoid this?

Appreciation starts with recognition. Talking and listening are the blood of a relationship; they need to flow to keep the relationship healthy. Sometimes raising issues is hard, but the more you talk, the easier it is. Friendships can fall without it; with your partner, it is even more essential.

The best way to keep the blood flow healthy is by maintaining a mutual appreciation, and you do this by being interested and being interesting. By being someone you'd want to be around; and by challenging your partner in this same way.

Consider these words by Kahlil Gibran in *The Prophet*:

> *Let there be spaces in your togetherness.*
> *And let the winds of the heavens dance between you.*
> *Love one another, but make not a bond of love:*
> *Let it rather be a moving sea between the shores of your souls.*
> *Fill each other's cup but drink not from one cup.*
> *Give one another of your bread but eat not from the same loaf.*
> *Sing and dance together and be joyous, but let each one of you be alone,*
> *Even as the strings of a lute are alone though they quiver with the same music.*
> *Give your hearts, but not into each other's keeping.*
> *For only the hand of Life can contain your hearts.*
> *And stand together, yet not too near together:*
> *For the pillars of the temple stand apart,*
> *And the oak tree and the cypress grow not in each other's shadow.*

'Grow not in each other's shadow' is about respecting each other's individuality. Respect has to be two-way. Yet mutual respect is founded on each person having self-respect. Why is this?

Consider a relationship with someone with low self-worth; it will be one-sided and dysfunctional. Someone who puts little value on themselves will value little when they give of themselves. If the gift is worthless, it is not appreciated; in fact, it will quickly become expected. This leads to decreasing respect from the receiver and decreasing self-respect in the giver. In this way do relationships sometimes deteriorate into darker places.

If, on the other hand, both people have a strong sense of self and there is mutual respect between the two, then when one asks, the other knows it is asked respectfully, and when one gives, the other knows that it is given freely by someone who has choice and is giving because they want to.

Is an 'unconditional' relationship the ultimate? No! A truly unconditional one is worthless. It means that a person can do whatever they like, and I'll still be there. They can lie, cheat, disrespect me, whatever, and I'll just let it go. That's not a relationship – it's abuse!

Conditionality may sound mechanical or transactional, but it isn't; as relationships establish and become more long-term, then conditions move from specific interactions to trust-based. In a meaningful relationship that is established over time, doing things for the other unconditionally is part of the strength and joy of that relationship. But that doesn't mean the relationship itself is unconditional, just that I expect nothing back from that specific act of giving. I know I get it back in other ways.

Children, if you have them, do require unconditional commitment during their formative years and this is the obligation and responsibility you take on in having them; but your job is to wean them off that dependency, to take ownership and responsibility for themselves and their own decision-making, just as you have been doing over these last few years.

Ultimately, you will get the relationships you deserve; this is, of course, a two-edged sword. People with strong values and principles will not put up with close friends with weak ones. It would betray those very values. In this way, you will find that strong, shared values are the greatest glue, as long as they are consistently applied. Of course, there will be imposters you come across but by being clear on your principles, you can root them out.

Strong friendships add an extra dimension to life. They can double your potential. They provide spark and colour to your life, inspiration and encouragement. Fun is better shared; people feed off each other, whether past stories or future dreams. Friends can be sounding boards but good ones will challenge you and be honest critics too. It can be lonely just inside your own head and friends and family are an exit, a perspective and a release valve from pressures that can build up.

The close relationships will be the ones you can laugh and cry with, talk to without pretence and in confidence, ask for help and know it will be answered. Boyfriends, ultimately husband/partner, will get to know you and share with you a unique intimacy; if you are lucky, your partner becomes your closest friend, your biggest fan and closest support, while still able to be critical, knowing their own self and being confident in it, as they should be. The hardest decision in life, perhaps; don't rush it.

Life is short; always take the time to reflect on who are the important people in your life and invest in them. Thousands of online 'friends' will never replace one good friend who has been there for you and come through. Setting high standards for relationships will not give you many close friends but, to take Cherry's words, they will not be 'shopkeepers' and 'that is worth a great deal'. It is indeed.

With my love,

Dad xx

8. What's Important

South Pole
15 December 2005

'*The Pole. Yes, but under very different circumstances from those expected.*'

The famous words from Captain Scott's diary on seeing that Amundsen had beaten him to the South Pole. They sit quietly on a sign at the South Pole commemorating his and Amundsen's epic journeys to the Pole, the first among mankind. And there I am in front of it. They don't just sit there, though; their silence fills the space around me. In that largest of wildernesses, the exploits of five men fill the atmosphere with electricity and intensity, the sunlight around me refracted by their presence.

***

Apsley Cherry-Garrard was a twenty-four-year-old who, through connections, got himself on to Scott's expedition to the South Pole. He had no polar experience or scientific knowledge to add, yet he played a huge part.

His book describes the whole expedition but the *Worst Journey in the World*, the title of his book, is the story of his winter foray with his two companions, Bill Wilson and 'Birdie' Bowers. Its power is enhanced by the senselessness of the journey – to collect some penguin eggs for scientific research.

In permanent darkness, temperatures down to -70 degrees C without wind chill, they get marooned in an igloo by a hurricane (they recorded it to force 11) with weeks still to travel to safety. Then they lose their tent, their only means of getting to safety:

'It was blowing as though the world was having a fit of hysterics. The earth was torn in pieces: the indescribable fury and roar of it all cannot be imagined.

I can well believe that neither of my companions gave up hope for an instant. They must have been frightened, but they were never disturbed. As for me, I never had any hope at all … What else could I think? We had spent days in reaching this place through the darkness in cold such as had never been experienced by human beings. We had been out for four weeks under conditions in which no man had existed previously for more than a few days, if that. During this time we had seldom slept except from sheer physical exhaustion, as men sleep on the rack; and every minute of it we had been fighting for the bed-rock necessities of bare existence, and always in the dark. We had kept ourselves going by enormous care of our feet and hands and bodies, by burning oil, and by having plenty of hot fatty food. Now we had no tent, one tin of oil left out of six, and only part of our cooker. When we were lucky and not too cold we could almost wring water from our clothes, and directly we got out of our sleeping-bags we were frozen into solid sheets of armoured ice. … Without the tent we were dead men. …

It was two days and two nights since we had had a meal. … We returned against the wind, nursing our faces and hands, and settled that we must try and cook a meal somehow. … Very slowly the snow in the cooker melted, we threw in a plentiful supply of pemmican, and the smell of it was better than anything on earth. … None of us ever forgot that meal …

We turned out to have a further search for the tent. … I followed Bill down the slope. We could find nothing. But as we searched, we heard a shout

62

somewhere below … We came upon Birdie with the tent … Our lives had been taken away and given back to us.'

***

14 December 2005

'*Coldplay, Kaiser Chiefs, Snow Patrol, Elbow, Oasis…*' I am talking to myself in my face mask. I can recite back the last twenty-five songs on my music player; it feels a small act towards keeping my sanity. There are four of us, in line, arching on our skis, harnesses taut from our shoulders and waists back to the battered orange pulks behind us. We edge ever forwards, hour after hour, the pulks bumping and sliding along the white and blue ice, like reluctant children. The sastrugi, small ridges created by the wind, require an extra lean forward and dig in with the ski poles; maintaining momentum is key. It never seems to end. There's no talking; you are there, cocooned inside your balaclava, mask and goggles, your consciousness floating inside.

The midnight blue sky has been replaced by whiteness; a giant opaque circle of light, from where the sun should be, is the only definition in front, the horizon of ice and mist fading into one. Definition is gone; we press on towards an invisible destination.

My mind drifts homewards. I can't get the words '*I've never been this far away from home*' from the Kaiser Chiefs' song out of my head. It makes me smile – I bet they weren't thinking of Antarctica when they wrote it. Then I turn to loved ones. What I would give for a Sunday lunch with my parents. I wonder what Kate is doing now. Life goes on at home… and I go forward on my little journey.

We pull up briefly for a break. I reach into my pulk for some snacks and water; I turn my back to the wind and hunch down to take down my face mask. It is stuck to my jacket, iced up by the winds and my breathing. I peel it, like a plaster, from my skin; my cheeks redden, despite the weeks of weathering. I never get used to the sharpness of the air; it steals your breath and bites your skin. It gets brutal with the slightest wind; there's nowhere to hide. It whistles from thousands of miles away, building momentum, a different kind of desert storm. I don't bother asking how cold it is any more, minus thirty, minus forty with wind chill maybe?

Ice chills my throat as I try to force down wooden chocolate and rapidly cooling water from a flask. Ten minutes' break and we have to get going; I'm starting to shiver. I didn't put an extra layer on and the sweat is cooling down my spine.

The mask has gone solid. I lift it back over the contours of my face, forcing its glacial form on to my already numb skin and iced-up beard. I ask one of the team to check that there's no skin showing between the mask and my goggles. I am already carrying blisters from a previous gap. Small acts of imprudence are disproportionately punished here.

Head down again and then push off, trying to glide as much as possible. The mind starts to wander off again into dreams, until the pulk gets stuck on a small ridge and jolts me back into consciousness. And so I wander between reality and fantasy, ambitions and annoyances, and the significant and the inconsequential.

Then there is a dot on the horizon; the GPS confirms our position. We are in sight of Scott's goal nearly a hundred years previously.

And then there is the sign.

The stories of Scott and his men fill my mind as I look around. It is easy to make legends of the dead but they can lift our sights. I wrote this in my diary:

> *In describing the beautiful harshness of his journey and the noble tragedies of Scott's, [Cherry] opened not just the myth of Antarctica for me, but some of the core realities of human existence. In my own incomparable way, I had now experienced some of the pain and privation of Cherry and the highs and lows of Scott. What a privilege.*

***

'Needs? I guess that is what bothers so many folks. They keep expanding their needs until they are dependent on too many things and too many other people...'

Sam Keith and Richard Proenneke, *One Man's Wilderness*

'It has been a long mental and physical haul. You have lots of time to yourself but it makes you appreciate what you have and understand what you need.'

'It is about trying to maximise the time spent on doing meaningful things with meaningful people.'

My diaries, Antarctica 2005

My Dear Kate,

In what direction(s) do you want to take your life? Whom do you want to spend your time with? How do you identify the significant over the minutiae in your day-to-day?

If you know what's important to you, it should be much easier to make such decisions.

This seems an obvious thing to say but it is amazing how few of us really invest the time to reflect on it. How many people only get to realise the importance of someone when they are gone, whether that's an undervalued partner or a departed relative or friend? How often is said, 'I wish I had told them…'? Similarly, in the seeming chaos of our day-to-day lives and the never-ending 'urgency' of the next meeting, call or activity, how many times do we say 'I wish I could have done that…' or 'You're so lucky to be able to do that…'? And how many get to the ends of long careers at work and ask what it was all for?

If we could only do meaningful things with meaningful people, then wouldn't we overcome this? Wouldn't life be full of meaning?

Yet life itself gets in the way. It is getting more complex, more demanding, faster. Media feeds wants we don't need, trying to keep up with neighbours we don't know, chasing dreams manufactured on TV, living a life increasingly exposed in real time on social media. This creates pressure. Pressure to respond, to be a part, pressure to conform, to earn and to spend. Information is ubiquitous, communication instantaneous, social media's presence all-intrusive, with no filter but the thumb; if we don't have some means of prioritising, then we can drown in the noise or drift with the fashion (I use this in the broadest sense of anything popular). All currents follow the paths of least resistance; it is often hard to swim against them.

66

This life gives little time to the self or to understand who and what are important to us. These are often things or people closest to us, where appreciation can get lost. But they can be things that we come upon during life; climbing and the wild in general have become very important to me over time, but they were nothing to me at your age. Some friends will be for life; others will come and go.

It is only with perspective that we see things for what they are.

If the reality that you know is what is in front of you, then the only way to do a check on it is to get outside it. At a mundane level, if you can leave your phone alone for some time, this can be as simple as taking the dog for a walk or going for a run; for some it is a quiet place, like a church. It is about good personal time inside your own head. However, the greater the physical and time separation, the greater will be the perspective and objectivity.

The best places that I have found for me to do this are in big landscapes, where I'm at once small but at the same time my mind can expand like the horizons in front of me. 'Appreciating what you have and understanding what you need' is part of a blog I read down a satellite phone, looking from my tent door across the Antarctic nothingness. There is no place on Earth like it to make one understand this; my smallness against its expanse, my frailty against its power, man's fragility against its timelessness. It forces reflection. Getting back to the basics of life helps with perspective; it helps isolate needs from wants, experiences from possessions, friends from acquaintances.

When I walk or cycle down a long path in the hills and return the same way, I see the surroundings differently coming back; I see new things for the first time and gain different perspectives on familiar landmarks. So it is after trips away; I return with new angles on my life at home, those dear to me, my work and my life outside work, the things I may be taking for granted and the things I may be getting too worked up about, what I can control and what I can't and what I should be prioritising and de-prioritising. I come back refreshed and focused. It is partly from the trip itself; the exercise, the outdoors air, the sleeping so close to the elements, but it is also driven by the time to consider, to ruminate, sometimes to daydream, sometimes even getting close to meditation. It is the breathing space I need when something has gone wrong or the reality check when things are flying high. It is not only a health or sanity check but a mental detox.

It doesn't have to be mountains or sea or ice, of course. Whatever environments you choose, it is about finding your own ways to get the perspective to untangle the congestion that can clog all our brains. As life gets more pressured and intrusive, isolating the meaningful from the minutiae gets more important. It is one of the keys to making the most out of your life.

Good luck!

Dad xx

9. The Two Journeys

Alaska 2005/6

Alaska – that place up in the far north-western corner of North America. Near-permanent darkness in winter, huge mosquitoes in summer, full of nothing but oil, fish and bears… and a lot of 'batshit crazy' people, to use some American vernacular.

Why would you bother going all that way for that?

***

Denali, camp 3, 14,200 feet
11 June 2006

I win the competition with 'Strongjaw and the Nuns of Dead Man's Creek'. What else are you going to do when you are snowed in on Denali? The first day maybe you'll do some personal chores, some cleaning, clear snow from your tent, maybe update the diary; the second, you read a book and clear snow. The third, you swap books and clear snow. Discussions and stories get more and more eclectic. Then the fourth, after you've cleared snow, you really are starting to go crazy. Will it ever break? Will we have enough supplies or time to have a go for the summit? Got to keep positive but it is howling outside and snow is whipping up in mini tornadoes around camp. The tent walls seem very tight.

So we have a short-story competition. For some reason known only to himself, Louis had picked up a Mills & Boon American equivalent in Anchorage, called *Longarm*; this is my inspiration for Strongjaw. It easily wins the short-story competition that day but I suspect will take no further prizes. It will remain locked away in my diary.

More of the same, wind whistling around camp blowing up clouds of snow… In the moments when the wind drops down here, you can hear the constant growl from the ridge above, like a stormy sea clattering on to shore. It must be miserable up there [at 17,200-foot camp] – already a few groups have come back down, one saying how the wind was actually knocking over snow walls up there! Another from the West Rib experienced winds gusting to 100 mph, they said. No time to be up high. Some are headed for home, either having had enough or not having enough food.

As we came up so quickly we have a few days [of food] in hand but that doesn't take away any of the frustration or monotony. A Chinese lady has just come down and is being treated for severe frostbite… And two very experienced female climbers are missing attempting a difficult route on Mt Foraker (adjacent to Denali), feared dead. It brings it home to you.

The winds abate for a while; the sun breaks through and suddenly untamed mountains stretch as far as the eye can see, glistening and shimmering before me. I sit down on an ice wall, and look to the horizon. And as my thoughts meander, I start to wonder what is going on in a different corner of Alaska.

I think back to travelling through Alaska with David W, and two old friends, Wendy and Karen, on a real American road trip through some of its legendary places, in a huge SUV and an ill-suited four-person tent that would singularly fail to meet the rigours of a Valdez gale and McCarthy rains…

A smile comes over my face.

Eastern Alaska, May 2005
Somewhere near McCarthy

Ow! My head smacked into David's. 'Don't drop it,' he shouted. We were covered in mud, sitting in the back of a beefed-up golf buggy, heading somewhere into the interior of Alaska, clutching a bottle of whisky. We had just had to get out in ankle-deep mud to attach a winch to a tree to haul the entrenched cart out of the mud. In our state, this had resulted in face plants and backflips into the bog.

Wendy and Karen found this very funny from the view of the cab of the cart; they just sat there, together with our new friend, Peggy, while we made fools of ourselves. Peggy knew Karen from a nursing locum job in Alaska and had travelled all the way cross country from her log cabin in the middle of nowhere to meet us in a pub in McCarthy, a town of around thirty people in eastern Alaska. McCarthy was born in a mining rush and still looked exactly like a wild west movie set. The pub, or perhaps saloon, was the only watering place in a long distance and the four of us had descended on it, to the bemusement of locals, in the late afternoon, to take refuge from the rains.

Peggy joined us later; she was pint-sized but beefy and red-cheeked; she exuded the no-nonsense air that is the way with people of the frontiers. She told stories of bears she had faced down with a nonchalance that captivated us. She offered to take us to her log cabin; she had bunks in the outhouse, apparently. 'What the hell...', 'Can't be any worse than our leaking tent in this weather' – a consensus arose. Alcohol may have coloured the decision as we had kept drinking through the evening to accompany Peggy's stories.

I have little recollection of the bunkhouse except that it was basic and we were dry. The next morning was hurting as we knocked on the door of the cabin. A giant of a man came to the door. 'Hi, I'm Scott,' he said in a slow, friendly drawl, pushing out his hand. He was Peggy's husband. He had a moustache and a couple of days' stubble, a green checked shirt and a fraying baseball cap; lean and broad-shouldered, his hands were the size of melons. While coffee brewed and the morning sun angled in through a window, we sat at the kitchen table in this vast cabin that they had built themselves.

As the first coffee kicked in, I became engrossed in their story. They lived off the land, except for kerosene (paid for by Peggy's locum work), which they hauled in on the cart. He fished salmon, hunted game and planted vegetables and they bottled or tinned and stored underground what they needed for the winter. He liked rugby. The work never stopped during the daylight months to cover for the perpetual darkness and cold of the winter, from dawn to dusk.

The four huskies suddenly started going wild outside, their chains cracking as they whipped tight. Something was in the neighbourhood… We went outside to check it out, Scott with his gun. The dogs fell silent. Whatever it was had cleared off.

I looked around. Huge forests sweeping over hills, a large river coursing through about half a mile away, the air crisp and cold, few sounds to break the purity of the moment, but the occasional rustlings of the huskies. And here we were in the middle of it all, a small plume of smoke rising from the cabin chimney the only sign of man across the horizons.

***

Denali summit 20,310 feet
16 June 2006

The summit ridge is in mist; the air is biting. Denali never warms, it seems. At times, it is hard to tell what is up or down, solid track or fall off to left or right. We are silent, in concentration. I take it very steadily, focusing on each step. I stop when Mike stops.

'We're here, guys. Nice work.' Mike puts out his hand.

My focus lifts. I look around; the views of yesterday are lost in the fog of today. I wouldn't know we had reached the top, but still the satisfaction is huge. All those days of preparation, of hauling sleds and packs, of waiting out storms, of grinding through snow drifts and up ice, have come to this.

Louis and I hug. We had worked for this one. The weather conditions sum up the climb itself, and Alaska.

Tough and unforgiving. A heck of a place to experience.

***

'Keep Ithaka always in your mind.
Arriving there is what you are destined for.
But do not hurry the journey at all.
Better if it lasts for years,
so you are old by the time you reach the island,
wealthy with all you have gained on the way,
not expecting Ithaka to make you rich.
Ithaka gave you the marvelous journey.
Without her you would not have set out.
She has nothing left to give you now.
And if you find her poor, Ithaka won't have fooled you.
Wise as you will have become, so full of experience,
you will have understood by then what these Ithakas mean.'

C.P. Cavafy, 'Ithaka', *Collected Poems*

'The more you live life, the better you get at it.'

My diaries, Chile 1996

My Kate,

The *Odyssey* is one of the most famous journeys in literature. Odysseus has a simple goal – to get home. Yet through a mixture of his own hubris and the people, gods, demi-gods and monsters he encounters along the way who deliberately or inadvertently change his course, his journey is far from simple. He takes ten years to get back, bouncing or blown from one encounter to the next.

The story has many relevancies still today. 'Life is a journey' is often quoted but really it is two. It has taken me a while to figure this out!

While I was travelling through Chile in 1996, I wrote: *'I have an extremely searching character which can be a strength and a weakness. For I haven't yet defined my scope; I keep on searching and experiencing.'* I was thirty-three and still 'searching'!

My diary exposes the issue: *'For those of us who are achievement orientated, once you have climbed the mountain, what do you do next? Climb a bigger one?'*

It had taken me a while to realise that I shouldn't be searching for anything in particular. The answers were in front of me. What I was doing was right but I was looking at it wrongly. There was nothing to search for. If I kept exploring, I would find things; if I had an open mind and heart, I would learn things.

I was getting closer to understanding what I had imprinted in my mind from all those years previously in my life, the words of the Delphic Oracle in Ancient Greece: 'gnothi seauton' or 'know yourself'. Life was a journey of discovery: a physical journey of discovery and an internal journey of personal discovery – and there was an intimate and symbiotic relationship between the two.

I have lived these two journeys. Both the physical experiences I
have been through and where I am now personally, I could not have
predicted when I was eighteen. I met Louis in Antarctica and that
led to Denali and then many other adventures. I got fascinated with
Peggy and Scott's lifestyle and bought a book, *One Man's Wilderness*, on
the way home. Both fostered trips into the wild and a desire to explore
the boundaries of such existences.

This has been a learning process for me – learning to keep my eyes
open, as much as anything, and not close my mind to the unfamiliar. I
know I closed off options too early in my twenties. I followed well-
trodden routes initially and didn't take the time to look at options in the
bigger picture and take bigger risks, which, in hindsight, wouldn't really
have been that risky at all. But I have grown by realising such things,
and that journey from the shy risk-averse teenager to today is as a
result of the experiences I've had and people I've met along the way.

Just as with Odysseus, the two journeys are about finding a balance
between staying on path and open-mindedness towards new
opportunities and between mental focus on tasks and absorption in
the experiences that, between them, bring fulfilment and dimension to
life. I have always had goals and ambitions but have learnt that they
are not the be-all and end-all, that life is full of twists and turns and I
need to be flexible enough to adjust to changes and happenings, both
the good and the bad.

From whatever base, in whatever direction, I know I am pushing my
understanding of self and my potential as long as I am consciously
pushing my comfort zone. The breadth and the depth of the
experiences on the way develop the personal journey of self-discovery;
at the same time, self-awareness fuels the experiences as the learning
and willingness and confidence to try things grow. Momentum is
worth a lot.

Unlike me, and I suspect many, you already have a clear desire and understanding of what you want to do as a career. I'm very happy for you on this; being a vet offers many opportunities and can be a very fulfilling and challenging path. You've still, though, got a journey through life to navigate and a journey as a vet. You've still got to make the what, where and how decisions; you could be a small animal vet in an English town, a horse vet in America or a wildlife vet in deepest Africa, or all three. It is the same with the rest of your life; you still have most of the chapters of your own book to write.

If you pursue the two journeys throughout life, as with Odysseus, you will be wealthy with all you have gained along the way. When you explore the boundaries of your capabilities and experience, even in a small way, you will return with new perspectives and new understanding; in some small (or maybe large) ways, you will have grown and your horizons, both internally and externally, will have stretched.

May they expand far!

Dad xx

10. Character

Round the World Sailing Race 2007/8

I am in the South China Sea, taking part in the Clipper Round the World (RTW) sailing race, nearly three thousand miles from the leg start in Singapore. A storm, gusting 40 knots, has scattered the fleet.

8 February 2008

The storm sail cracks like a whip. It's a shuddering noise above even the gale that is whistling through the rigging and the dark seas that are pounding the decks, angry at our impertinent presence. A sheet [rope] has snapped and the sail flaps free like a dragon tail back and forth across the foredeck; we know the drill but it doesn't make it any easier. We've got to get it down and fast. Jen reaches for the other sheet to winch it in and I go for the halyard to let the sail down.

The snake pit is a nest of ropes; we're scrambling in the lurching of the boat and the drowning waves of water that intermittently engulf us to keep our feet and keep momentum. There's a shout from further back.

'What the **** are you playing at? Get the ****ing sail down.' The bark of our skipper, Dougie, coming up behind us, his energy and presence belying his slight frame. He never lets up.

I want to say back, 'What the **** do you think we're trying to do?' but that's stupid, just get on with it, I tell myself.

I pass the halyard to Jen, unclip my safety and move forward, grasping for the next runner to clip into. I crawl up on to the deck and stagger like an old drunk, trying to move with the motion of the boat as it rolls sideways and then crests a big wave and hurtles like a big dipper down the other side. I spit out mouthfuls of water as I grasp the stay and cling to it. Falling to my backside, my legs either side of the stay, I reach up for the sail. My hands are cold; the sail, slippery like wax paper, flashes side to side, kicking back at my attempts to get it under control. The hacks are iced up, numbing my fingers further. I grit my teeth and shout into the wind as I give an almighty heave on them. It's coming. A big wave pours over my back and down my neck and then washes up the deck, up my waterproofs, filling my boots. Iced water down to my core but I don't give it a thought. What do you think about when you have a monster by the tail?

Someone is coming up with another sheet to attach; I can't make out who with the hood up, the seas stinging my eyes. As we maul over the clew, I see the dark eyes of Dougie. 'C'mon Paul, let's get this done.'

I'm panting to hold the sail while he threads the rope to tie the bowline. No room for error. Adrenalin rushes through… I'm fighting with all my energy to keep hold of the sail while on a slippery deck at thirty degrees, as the bow cuts into the next wave. I try to get a foot into the base of a rail. If I lose hold, the sail could catch either of us in the face. It flashes through my mind and back out. Dougie's face is contorted with strain and focus.

'Let's get back,' he shouts, 'let's get this thing sailing again.' The race drives us on. Minutes could matter for our position. We scramble back to the snake pit to hoist the sail again.

Then I go flying.

I try to get a grip of myself and my safety line. I'm seeing stars literally in front of my eyes, like a cartoon character, except there's no humour. I've just been thrown across the snake pit, banged my head on a winch and been flung sideways. The clip on my safety harness judders me back in the opposite direction, just as the boat lurches over, a wave gust driving it to leeward. We get the halyard fixed and the sheet winched in. The brutal cracking of the sail abates – for now.

I work my way back to the cockpit, gingerly, carefully unclipping and clipping my safety in. Dougie is back, staring at the screen below.

'Dougie, I've banged my head on a winch, not feeling great.' I point to my head.

His unshaven, gaunt face, hollowed by lack of sleep, squints through the half-light to where my finger points. A lump is developing on the side of my head.

'Go take a rest, Paul,' in his soft Scottish accent that always hid the steel behind, 'should be fine in the morning.'

I don't argue – these aren't conditions to mess with – but I'm not sure how much sleep I'll get.

I take off my wets in the saloon and hand-walk my way towards the bow, pushing back against the pitching of the boat. In our group cabin, I strip further to my base layer, and wait for the next dive of the boat to pull myself into my bunk. I force damp socks into my flattened sleeping bag. Exhaustion pushes me to sleep but the constant pounding and rolling of the boat tests the extremities. Wetness is a condition of existence here; a salty wetness from sea and sweat that is everywhere and in everything. No hatches open with the sea continuously washing the decks above, so the smells of nineteen days on board are trapped in the cabin that is our spartan home when not on watch.

Spare sails stacked around our bunks, steam rising from our bodies and our breathing, condensing on the cabin roof and dripping back down into our bunks. I am violently rolled into the side of the boat, the only thing that separates me from the sea outside, banging my head as the boat lifts, hangs and then crashes down into the water.

Then the call comes from above for a change of tack and just as the guys on watch above jump to their positions for the final 'ready-about' shout, so we drag our bodies out of our bunks and move our damp bags to the other side of the cabin to try to get some sleep on the high side of the boat. It doesn't happen. Drifting, banging, rolling…

10 February
Missed a day of diary due to storm tiredness – gusting well over 40 [knots]
apparent at times with very big seas.

By morning I was fine, though sporting a decent lump on the side of my
head. Everyone has bumps and bruises over them – it is a fact of life in
these conditions. Yesterday's day shift was one of the most tiring experiences
of my life; as soon as I got on deck, one of the staysail sheets broke again
and we had to get it down so I was straight up on to the foredeck. Two hours
into the watch I thought I had done a day's work; reefing main, tacks and
fixing the various problems as they arose.

Helming was a great experience – [other] people didn't want to get on
it. For me it was one of the things I wanted to experience on this trip –
helming in a storm… big seas, waves up to maybe 50 metres from peak
to trough, and a lot of crashing of the bow into them. At times it felt
like a rollercoaster. I loved it and apparently I did pretty well at it – even
Dougie commented – despite the barrage of waves and rain and hail, eyes
permanently flickering, like windscreen wipers in overdrive… As ever, the
tougher it gets, the closer you get to the basic survival requirements and other
refinements go out of the window.

Qingdao, 15 February
There will be an intensity gap initially on leaving the boat. An intensity of
everything – the proximity of living, the closeness of everyone, especially on
your watch and your reliance on them for your safety in many circumstances,
the intensity of the racing, whether the pressure on helming to get the
numbers or pressures on sail changes or manoeuvres, whether from the skipper
or what you put on yourself. There will be a bit of 'bubble bursting' that is
no bad thing. As the intensity of the memories fades, there will be a glow
of satisfaction. I will go back with energy and enthusiasm to get stuck into
things at home, work and play. And I will be plotting the next adventure.

It was never going to be a life-changing experience – I wasn't looking
for one and it would mean I was doing something wrong before, if it was.
All I want from these trips is to push my comfort zone further, extend my

knowledge of self and my worldly experiences – essentially a self-evolution. You don't get that by sitting behind a desk, however interesting your work. Work does provide mental challenge and satisfaction in its own right and undoubtedly some of my work experiences have contributed significantly to my personal development – especially the less successful ones! – but in terms of testing your spirit, your strength of mind and your moral fortitude (true colours shine through under extreme pressure), nothing compares to these sorts of trips.

When I think of MacArthur or Slocum, or Cherry or Scott, it makes my own small efforts seem paltry, but everything is relative to circumstances and conditions. Despite the relative inadequacies of my trips, they have done a lot to make me who I am today. I will continue to be inspired in such ways. Somehow nature brings purity to the human condition.

***

'It does not really matter much whether your man whose work lies in or around the hut shirks a bit or not, just as it does not matter much in civilisation: it is just rather a waste of opportunity. But there's precious little shirking in Barrier sledging; a week finds most of us out.'

Apsley Cherry-Garrard, *The Worst Journey in the World*

Dear Kate,

My sailing started in Abersoch as a kid in my summer holidays. I
started with Popa in a dinghy, much like you and I did, though I would
like to think I had a bit more experience when I took you out than
when he and I first spent half our time in the water trying to right our
capsized Laser in the freezing North Wales waters. From there I raced
some larger boats and did a number of Mediterranean and Caribbean
sailing holidays; I could crew a boat well enough, though I had had no
technical training. It was enough to get accepted into the Clipper race
programme and I signed up for the legs from South Africa to Australia
to Singapore to Qingdao. In the three weeks training beforehand, it
felt quite a big step up technically but not from a 'pushing self' point
of view… just a different way of pushing self. Working closely in a new
team and taking orders from a skipper were challenges for me!

It is an interesting dynamic when you step into a new environment
like a racing boat, barely knowing the other crew or the skipper. I
tend to keep my peace. I've always believed that, especially in physical
situations, actions speak much louder than words. I feel that if I follow
a dictum of 'under-committing and over-delivering', then I will build
trust and confidence in those around me. I try to let time run its course.
I'm not afraid to admit ignorance or ask for help or admit to messing
up. But I try damn hard not to ask twice or mess up a second time!

Those that talk a good game are often the ones found most wanting
later. I refer to this in my diary on the trip. The tiredness and physical
demands of the storm in the South China Sea exposed many souls!
As Cherry said, ordinary life doesn't do this; we have too many
facades, or excuses, or avoidances. This is why we can get let down by
others. They haven't been truly tested, or their characters exposed,
and then something happens that really does challenge them, and
they are found wanting.

Character is what a friend who was involved in SAS recruitment called 'hearts and minds'. Not many of us have the 'hearts and minds' necessary to get into the SAS but, in my experience, many have characters that they have neither really tested nor developed.

Character is about values, for sure. But it is more than that. Character is what is left when the music stops, when there's nothing to hide behind, when we're so beaten-up or pressured that the real self comes out – when how we act defines who we really are.

Can we develop our character? I suspect SAS recruitment would say not. Maybe to their level of expectation they are right. But otherwise, I think it is possible, if we do it consciously. It requires a willingness to stand on Thoreau's deck and expose ourselves. But this can be done gradually.

You've got to want to not let yourself down, or your colleagues, when it feels like all you want to do is pack it in. It will take gritted teeth but when you've stood strong in a gale or two, you know you can take the next one on, and then you can stand tall when life throws other things at you.

Courage, as the French say!

Love always,
Dad xx

11. Serendipity

Batam Island 2009

Java Sea off Indonesia
16 January 2008

I couldn't sleep. The humidity was turning our cramped berths into saunas in the morning sunshine; coming off that 2 a.m. to 6 a.m. watch and then trying to sleep was always the worst one.

Initial tiredness put me out but then I woke in a pool of sweat. The boat was gently rolling with the spinnaker, the sea comfortingly sloshing down its hull, next to my head, but that didn't help. I decided to get up.

I wandered into the saloon to get some water and check out how we were doing. Justin was quietly getting on with preparing lunch in the galley, the conditions far more helpful than the forty-five-degree angle when it had last been my turn to be cook.

'Couldn't sleep?' He knew what it was like. I nodded. 'Coffee?'

'Great,' I said, 'thanks,' picking up a tattered *National Geographic* on the seating.

'"Dangerous Straits".' I read the cover title out aloud.

'Yeah, you know that's where we are heading?' Justin laughed. I looked puzzled.

'Malacca Straits. See, look at the subtitle,' he pointed.

I read the next line: '"Pirates haunt it. Sailors fear it. Global trade depends on it." What the ****. So we're sailing up there?'

***

As we docked in a smart gated resort on Batam Island that was to be our home for a few days' rest, to a welcome from traditional Indonesian dancers and crates of beer, I shoved the magazine into my bag. It was, after all, a pirate base, according to *Nat Geo*.

After the first twenty-four hours of finding our land legs, washing, partying and sleeping, we discussed a trip into the town of Batam. The resort manager, a smiley chap with dainty features and the engaging name of Sweet-Pea, volunteered to take us; we hired a minibus for the next evening.

As we boarded the bus, Sweet-Pea welcomed us and proudly started extolling the riches of Batam. A lot of money seemed to have gone into the place.

Out through the security barriers, Sweet-Pea directed the van onwards. Corrugated-roofed huts housing families, shops and food stalls lined the road. People milled around, chatting or just staring out into the street; dogs slept on the pavements, chickens pecked at scraps. After a while, the road started improving and we came into a town of brand-new buildings and to the front door of a gilded hotel, lights ablaze.

Sweet-Pea ushered us out of the bus and through the rotating doors. The foyer was huge and golden. And it was empty but for a few staff in dark suits, quietly busying themselves.

He took us downstairs to a polished bar area; we became the only audience for the Indonesian band at the front, playing Beatles' covers. It was all a bit surreal – this huge, gaudy, empty hotel in the middle of nowhere, with a mispronounced 'It's been a hard day's night' the only life apparent.

We bought a round to be polite and chuckled at our situation.

'Where is everyone, Sweet-Pea?' someone asked. He waffled and changed the subject to how nice the hotel was.

'We need a place with some life to it, Sweet-Pea,' said Mike. Everyone concurred. We finished up.

Back on the bus, I pulled out the *Nat Geo* copy and pointed to a bar called Dynasty in there; it was where pirates went to drink. His face went ashen: 'No, no, too dangerous,' he said. Buoyed by a few beers, we overruled him.

On entering the club, we saw a bored barman leaning against a small bar, staring at a giant screen on the wall playing a music video of two Indonesians crooning a love song in softened light; the sound over the speakers was unsynced and appalling. Scanning the room, the reason became apparent to our left; a small moustached man was singing into a microphone, switching his gaze between the screen and the girl on the sofa next to him. They were alone in the bar; he didn't stop or seem perturbed by our entrance and I certainly was not going to suggest a change of tune. He wasn't wearing a skull and crossbones, but you never know.

Above a doorway leading into another area, there were lightbulbs beneath numbers, which occasionally flicked on and off. No one came or went through the bar but there was clearly activity going on elsewhere. The bored barman paid no attention to that or us, though he eventually agreed to serve us tins of beer. Sweet-Pea was agitated and twitchy.

The pirate finished up, the screen froze and Mike, with a cheeky smile said, 'Let's ask for "New York, New York"!' Sweet-Pea wasn't happy.

'C'mon, Sweet-Pea, it's the name of our boat. We've got to do it,' Jen said. Mike went to the pirate and politely asked to borrow the microphone.

He neither scowled nor smiled, just blankly handing the instrument over. Three of us got on stage and massacred Frank Sinatra's paean to our boat; of course, it seemed like great fun at the time. It was when the music stopped, as they say, that the silence became a little more uncomfortable.

The pirate was scowling; he shouted at the barman. The screen immediately switched back to Indonesian MTV. I don't know what was said but Sweet-Pea looked like he was about to pee. Enough was maybe enough.

We left our beers on the bar and headed for the door. Sweet-Pea took us directly to the resort, and never discussed the matter again.

I still have the karaoke slip from the bar in my diary, or at least I think that's what it was for.

***

'... while he is sound of limb, free from disease, untouched by suffering, the father of fair children and himself of comely form; and if in addition to this he shall end his life well, he is worthy to be called that which thou seekest, namely a happy man; but before he comes to his end it is well to hold back and not to call him yet happy but only fortunate.'

Herodotus, *The Histories*, Book 1 [32]

Dear Kate,

The ancient world, in particular the world of the Greeks of the fifth century BC, has had a big impact on my life. From having it practically beaten into me in earlier schooling to the fascination and challenge of university, the ideas and beliefs of this amazing period in history have come to be a part of me. From the epic landscapes and characters of Homer to the glorious stories of Herodotus, to the satire of Aristophanes and the turgid choruses of Aeschylus to the discourses of Socrates and the orations of Pericles, these writings came alive in my hands. As I studied how the Greeks discussed the condition of man, so I, in my ringside seat, was infused with their words, reflecting on the lot of man, the fragility of our existence and the search for meaning and purpose.

'Call no man happy till he is dead' was a typically Ancient Greek view of life. Probably the most famous story in this regard was told by Herodotus about a conversation between Solon and Croesus. Croesus, the king of Persia, asked the Athenian lawmaker who was the happiest man on Earth, expecting Solon to say of course that it was him, as he was the wealthiest and most powerful man. When Solon gave the names of some relative nobodies who had lived and died well, quoting the above refrain, Croesus was upset – but when his son was killed, his wife committed suicide and he had lost his kingdom to Cyrus, he had to reassess!

The Ancient Greeks put the randomness and luck of life down to the randomness and will of their gods, whom they depicted as more human than humans: jealous, mean-spirited, easily slighted, vain, prone to anger and vengeance and unaccountable except to a fickle father, Zeus, whose favour could be won more easily than a sub-Saharan dictator. Herodotus displays a typical Ancient Greek response to this: *'Far better is it to have a stout heart always, and suffer one's share of evils, than to be ever fearing what may happen.'* (Book 7 [50])

On the one hand, this could be seen as a fairly dour view on life; on the other, a realistic reflection on its vicissitudes. Since the Ancient Greeks lived, we have discovered a lot more explanations for the seemingly random events that happen to us; but even if we can explain the random better, it can still have a big effect on our lives, especially the bad things, what we often call 'bad luck'. Should we just be stoic, as Herodotus suggests?

The random or inexplicable can be a proxy for lack of knowledge or a lack of preparation or a lack of taking responsibility.

If I go to sea without checking the weather and without preparing contingencies, then is it bad luck or lack of care when a situation becomes critical because I haven't prepared? In practice, of course, it is impossible to take out all risk or foresee every eventuality. But if I have sailed all my life, then I will get better at reading signs and knowing how to deal with situations. Joshua Slocum, the first person to solo circumnavigate the world, concluded his book with these words:

'But above all to be taken into account were some years of schooling, where I studied with diligence Neptune's laws, and these laws I tried to obey.'

The more we have seen and done, the less what we come across will be a surprise. Gary Player, a famous South African golfer renowned for his work ethic, when told by a commentator about a lucky shot, replied that it was funny how the more he practised, the luckier he got. Understanding what is in our control and taking responsibility for it is important. It can be too easy to blame or assign cause to external events or people, in order to deflect personal responsibility.

However, we can also do the opposite. Not reflect enough on the randomness of life and accept that things happen the whole time that are unexpected and out of our control. Whether it is an act of nature or as a result of the busyness or complexity of modern life, things collide – atoms, people, cars, tectonic plates, some randomly, some predictably, some with forethought but not foresight. Rationalising the random as a part of our everyday life is essential to dealing with its vicissitudes.

'We make our own luck' is not said without reason. Attitude makes a huge difference; how many stories are there of those who have turned a bad event into a positive by the actions they subsequently take – the person made redundant from their job who goes on to set up their own business or the person disabled in a car accident who goes on to be a Paralympian. The glasses we view life through have a big effect on how bad 'bad' really is.

Over a very small period of history, the Ancient Greeks developed the foundations of much of our modern democracy, philosophy, architecture and literature. They had the right attitude; they understood the randomness of life but didn't let that stop them getting on with it and achieving some amazing things. And you shouldn't either.

Just be careful following up on random magazine articles.

With love,

Dad xx

12. What Risk?

Everest base camp
7 May 2009

You get used to the rumbles and growls of avalanches at Everest base camp. They are an intermittent yet constant reverberation in your ears and tremor in your stomach. They wake you at night, menacing the dark air.

But this was different.

This boomed. I left my notebook and rushed out of the mess tent. I could sense the tension in the air as others did the same. A huge snow cloud was developing on the icefall as a large block of ice and snow cascaded off the face of Lola to the left. It was all so fast. I heard a cry of 'Oh my god' from somewhere. The cloud kept growing, our visibility getting eclipsed by a storm of crystals, their refracted sparkle darkening the skies. It was mushrooming towards us, a half mile away. Flicks of ice on my face and then it was gone; sunshine restored. Thirty seconds, maybe a minute, that was all. I opened my eyes. It was different, the icefall.

I started to think rather than react. A few of our expedition party were up the mountain.

'Where's Regen?' someone asked, beside me. Regen was a member of our expedition party, a thin Quebecois of around fifty; he was a strong climber, always one of the quicker people up each stage. But yesterday he had started developing problems in his chest at camp 2 so he was coming down the mountain to be checked up.

The frailty of it all.

Radios immediately ignited, everyone trying to check up on their climbers and Sherpas; we knew Regen was on his way down – where was he? Minutes later, his radio crackled into life. He had missed the heart of the fall; but it soon turned out some others were missing so a number of groups began to mount rescue trips into the fall. Three people had been knocked down a crevasse – an Austrian guide and a client and a Sherpa. In time, help managed to pull out the guide and client; though hypothermic, they would survive, but the only signs of the Sherpa were, somewhat spookily, a boot and a pack. I'm guessing he wasn't clipped into the fixed ropes but I could be wrong. They continued the search for nearly three hours before they abandoned it.

We sat in the mess tent in silence listening to the radio unfold the stories and waiting for Regen to get down. Finally he arrived, shock all over his face and in every move he made. He and his Sherpa were yards away from the crevasse that the others had got caught in. They had managed to run and hide behind a large serac. The storm of snow and ice had as a result flown over their heads but he said he felt like he couldn't breathe for a while, the air was so thick with the avalanche. It ended up covering the ground with six to twelve inches of snow and ice – in a minute. The rescue mission had then begun.

Regen, back at base camp, was taken to the clinic; his shock at his near miss on the fall was more real than the chest pain at that point. He was adamant that he was on his way home. Still, he was diagnosed with angina by the doctors, so he had had two lucky escapes. I've just got back from the mess tent, where he was sat recounting and reflecting with an oxygen pipe coming out of his nose. His brother had died four months earlier and he was saying maybe it was him who had protected him today; he was close to tears as the shock wore off. He would be in Kathmandu tomorrow and home soon thereafter. Two days ago, he was practically running past us on a hike we were doing.

The loss of someone on the fall and the proximity of Regen's experience has hit us all. Has our risk changed? It has certainly become more real. It's like being punched in the stomach and then getting up looking for your corner, looking for an answer, when you know there isn't one. You have to make your own decision, pulled in two directions. As a result of someone else's misfortune today, the risk for us is less tomorrow, by how much I can't say. We are due to go up tomorrow. We will look stupid if we get caught in the same place but if we turn back now, it's all such a waste…

The south face of Everest has the unpredictable Khumbu Icefall as its start. It is like a giant bowl of ice cubes (part of it is actually called the Popcorn Field); it needs many ladders to navigate over crevasses and up ice walls, which are in constant need of rearranging due to the continuous ice movement. When you go through it, which you have to do typically six times on a summit bid, you are at risk from ice fall in the glacier itself and from avalanches from the abutting mountains.

But I knew this before I made the trip. I knew what the percentages were and I knew the best ways to mitigate the risks. This is why I carried on after the Regen incident.

***

'I would rather be ashes than dust!
I would rather that my spark should burn out in a brilliant blaze than it should be stifled by dry-rot.
I would rather be a superb meteor, every atom of me in magnificent glow, than a sleepy and permanent planet.
The proper function of man is to live, not to exist.
I shall not waste my days in trying to prolong them.
I shall use my time.'

Jack London, *Jack London's Tales of Adventure*

'You miss 100 percent of the shots you never take.'

Wayne Gretzky, ice hockey star

Dear Kate,

My teenage experiences of mountains peaked on the summit of Snowdon, much the same as you. My first 'big' mountain was more of a hike – up Kilimanjaro; Everest, at the time, was a distant place of gods and myths but one that got more real and present as I climbed closer to its heights.

There were risks on Everest, of course, when I attempted it, but they were considered ones.

On the way up to Everest base camp, I wrote: *'An Acceptable Risk (once you've done all you can to mitigate 'known' risk) is one where you are pushing your comfort zone but not shattering it; one that extends your knowledge and experience base, but doesn't leapfrog it. I believe Everest fits that description for me.'*

There are two sides to the risk equation: what is in my control and what is not. What is in my control is my knowledge and skill base. Do I have the technical skills and experience to tackle the route? I can take lessons in Scotland to develop my skills and climb other mountains to enhance my knowledge base.

What is also in my control is what I do before and during the trip to minimise, mitigate and contingency plan things that are outside my control, like the weather, mountain conditions and my health and fitness.

Just as Slocum described his voyage, I felt Everest was *'a natural outcome not only of my love of adventure but of my lifelong experience'*. I felt I had done my apprenticeship. I had trained hard and read much of others' experiences. I was climbing with a trusted friend and a guide I knew and who had summited before. I made a promise to Ana and you that I would follow his words, even if they were against my own mind and heart. We all agreed strategies to mitigate the risks on the mountain, like always climbing early in the morning when the ice is hard and snow more stable. We had a good weather-forecasting service and we followed it, not fought it. Just as Slocum, we tried to respect the laws of the mountain and not dismiss them.

You can calculate the accident rate on a road by dividing accidents into number of journeys. You can do the same with the icefall on Everest. What the road statistics don't break down into are the percentages when people were driving tired, or too fast because they were late for a meeting or were taking a phone call, or of those who went out on black ice to get a pint of milk. We can take risks for trivia without thinking, yet dismiss other risks without knowledge.

It is only with the unforeseeables that little can be pre-thought. In such events, it falls to experience and character. These are what you build by pushing your boundaries in the first place. The more experiences you have had, the more you'll have to draw on when unknowns happen; the more you've tested your character, the more it will stand true when pushed. Even with the unforeseeables, you can do much to de-risk.

Slocum's advice: *'To young [people] contemplating a voyage, I would say go. … Dangers there are, to be sure, on the sea as well as on the land, but the intelligence and skill God gives to man reduce these to a minimum.'*

Taking risks or not is the difference between living and existing, as Jack London says. The key is learning to take calculated ones.

Love always,
Dad xx

13. Dealing with Failure

Everest

23 March 2009

'*Sign here.*' The guy from Tigress Productions pointed to the bottom of the page. They were filming an Everest series for Discovery and our expedition company had signed up to it. I hadn't seen any of the previous series but they seemed like good guys. Still, if we were willing to be a part of it, we had to sign our rights away.

I looked at Louis and he shrugged. It all seemed a long way off, in the Kathmandu heat and bustle.

'What the hell,' I thought. We both signed.

***

Everest camp 3

18 May

'It could be your heart.' In an instant, in those five words, I know my shot at the summit is over. I try to argue with Scott. He doesn't have any medical kit with him, of course; he's just going off my brief description of symptoms. 'It could be anything,' I blurt.

I had just got up the Lhotse Face to camp 3; I wasn't myself, for sure. It had been easier the previous time on the acclimatisation rotation up here; it wasn't altitude sickness but my chest was a bit tight and I was breathing harder than I'd have liked. I had mentioned it to Mike, our guide, thinking it'd just be a case of a cup of tea and half an hour's rest; he'd asked Scott to take a look.

And here we are; tension shrinks my small tent. Steam is rising from our bodies and breathing; flashes of bright sunshine flick through the tent flaps.

'Please call the doctors at base camp, they checked me out before I came up.' I look at Scott; I know it is a long shot but I'm desperate. I am not thinking quickly; altitude and tiredness weigh on me. Base camp confirm what I have said, but aren't going to argue with someone on the mountain. I am done. They are sending me down.

As the first tear runs down my cheek, I notice the Discovery cameraman at the tent entrance. For a second, I think 'Great, this is how I'm going to be seen…' But I can't hold the tears and I don't really care. It hurts – a dream shattered and years of following and months of preparation gone in a flick of a radio button. Mike takes control. Not even a cup of tea. 'We'd better get you down, Paul. I'm sorry.' My throat is dry. I look at Louis; I can even see some glistening in his eyes. We've been through a lot together to get here and now he's continuing up. And I'm not.

We step outside the tent; no one says much. I guess there's little to say. Mike has organised a Sherpa to take me down on oxygen. So this is how my oxygen is going to get used.

I want to say I don't need the oxygen, to show I'm OK, that I shouldn't be going down. But I am going down. And I paid for the bloody stuff, so I may as well use it. My head is spinning with anger and desolation. I put the oxygen bottle into my pack; a final look at Louis. We hug.

'Good luck, mate' is all I can get out; my stomach is still a tight ball of emptiness. I shake hands with Mike and a few others, put on the mask and within minutes, they are small dark spots above me.

That simple. The end of my climb. I hadn't done anything wrong; I had been healthy all the time up to that point and the first time I complain of something, it was like my head being cut off; it's not me, I don't get sick, I've got a mountain to climb. But of course, they were right; with the available information, I needed to go down. I had promised before the trip that I wouldn't take stupid risks, that I would follow the experts' advice (though I was mainly thinking of my guide).

It was emotional for both Louis and me as we hugged; I think he was as shocked as I was. He had been sick several times on the way, I had not, but he was going up and I wasn't. That was that. But he has been a great friend throughout and there was no begrudging there; having said the farewells and good lucks, there was no looking back; there couldn't be. I trudged out of camp, like an invalid, oxygen mask on. What a turnaround; what a shock.

Base camp: afternoon of 18 May
I was taken straight to the HRA doctors at BC. The doctor, a jovial and experienced person whom I liked, got straight to the point and took the wind straight from my sails.

'You probably feel fine,' he said, 'and my tests will all be OK.'

Of course, he was right on both counts. BUT, of course, that didn't take away from what I had experienced at camp 3 and the equipment at base camp was not adequate to take the diagnosis any further. I asked him about my chest theory and he said it was very possible but it all had to be tested and that meant leaving. I asked him about my GI theory and he said it could be a part of the issue but not the whole.

'So that's a "no" to going back up then?' I asked.

'There's a chopper coming in for two other climbers in an hour, we may be able to get him to pick you up too.' I guess he was used to puncturing dreams.

That was it; decision made. We hastened back to my tent to pack my things and then to the helicopter pad. By this stage, my interview with the Discovery team was a little more reflective and rational, though when bells were being rung or pots clanged in recognition of a climber summiting up above, it did bring home what I had got so close to and yet fallen so far short. Mike and Louis were making good progress to camp 4, Mike's voice occasionally crackling over the radio to indicate the next milestone they had reached.

***

Final diary entry
So how do I feel? I've always said that life is a journey and that the experience of 'doing' is much the most important thing. But that feeling of pressure on your summit push when you know it all boils down to this, the concentration involved and the mental test, and finally that feeling when you've got to the top and you look down on the whole world below, I have missed all that.

Worse, I always knew I might not summit; it would be exceptionally arrogant to assume otherwise. But I always thought it would be me that would make that decision, that I would have given it my best shot but, for whatever reason, I could go no further. That was my promise to myself and it was taken from me. Not that I blame anyone; the decisions were right with the information available. A tiny part of me even hopes for some problem to be found to help vindicate them, though I feel confident there won't be anything serious and it will be just one of those unfortunately timed pieces of bad luck that had bigger implications than it would at any other time.

So I wait for tomorrow's helicopter early in the morning; I should be flying to a hot bath in Kathmandu and a cold beer at the same time as Mike and Louis are summiting. [Mike did summit, but Louis didn't, though he came back the following year and did it.]

I have found this in an earlier diary entry on the way up:
'There are many reasons to climb Everest; there are many more to come back down safely.' It doesn't feel quite like that as I sit alone in the mess tent at base camp.

***

'Examine the lives of the best and most fruitful people and ask yourself whether a tree that is supposed to grow to a proud height can dispense with bad weather and storms.'

Nietzsche, *The Gay Science*

***

My Dear Kate,

One of life's twisting knives is that the more you invest in an endeavour, the more you increase your chances of success, but so too do you increase the impact if you don't succeed. Everest was decades in the dreaming and reading, a seemingly impossible icon in the heavens at first, a couple of years in the planning, many months in the training, and then eight weeks away itself, away from you and Ana and from work during the post-crash stress of 2009. It was a sacrifice and a commitment. And it ended in a five-minute decision.

I was raw for a while afterwards.

The word 'failure' has such negative connotations. Failure in whatever form shines a light on us, whether the light comes from us ourselves, in questioning ourselves and our abilities, or it comes from the outside, by people who, to a greater or lesser degree, were a witness to the failure.

If we have wanted to achieve something, and it has not worked out, then that investment of time, energy and emotion may seem wasted, even foolish perhaps. Failure can hurt; it can bruise, it can affect self-confidence and it can attract criticism, cynicism or even mockery. Why go through anything that risks those? If I haven't tried, I will never have failed.

For this reason, fear of failure is one of the biggest deterrents to us fulfilling our dreams and ambitions and even a fraction of what we are capable of. The more fearful we are, the less we are willing to attempt.

Theoretically rationalising the idea of failure is quite easy. A big part of taking the fear out is learning to deal with it; while not making it something to get used to, it is an occasional and largely unavoidable consequence of the exploring soul. If we attempt things, some will not work out, plain and simple. Rationalising the process takes out the irrationality of the fear.

I have learnt to be selective in whom I listen to. Sometimes a deaf ear helps! But otherwise, I try to remember that ultimately the only person I have to justify myself to is me. Sometimes it is hard to be objective, so I may listen to experts for technical help, or listen to those who know me well for support.

Should you concern yourself with the opinions of people who are neither experts nor know you well? Criticism of your reading by an illiterate? You would laugh; so why worry about the uninformed opinion? If it is a technical comment, then it has no value. If it is a comment on effort, then you know better. If it is criticism simply that you tried, remember that those are usually the ones who have attempted little themselves.

I have learnt also the importance of reflection and context; not only is this how I learn from the experience but it is how I move on. When I got back from Everest, I saw several doctors back in the UK, and, after having every heart test available, it was clear my heart was in good fettle and of course, as I no longer had symptoms to analyse, no doctor could point to any alternative; 'things happen at altitude' was about the best I got.

As I reflected on the conditions of that early morning on the Lhotse face, I remembered the strong winds and swarming ice flakes chilling and tickling my lungs. I asked whether that could have triggered my asthma and the answer was possibly yes. I have since always carried inhalers with me and used them every time I climb. Whether it is coincidence, I don't know, but it has not happened since.

It is rare that reasons are simple; there are usually many variables, whether dealing with nature or dealing with people or just seemingly random events. In the aftermath, we can be too quick to blame ourselves or too quick to blame others. Sometimes all it needs is some quiet time to self, on a run or walk, but sometimes distance and time are required. I needed that for Everest.

When considering the variables, I try to isolate known unknowns from unknown unknowns; weather is a known unknown, but an earthquake? Louis went to Lhotse in 2015 and was lucky to avoid the terrible earthquake then, high up the mountain at camp 2. There's little to learn from the incident itself, it is so rare, except how he dealt with the situation overall. But ones like my chest on Everest can be learnt from for the next time. Considering what is in my control and what is not helps me isolate the variables and what I could have done something about. Rationalising is key to turning the page.

But the most important part of moving on has nothing to do with reflection and analysis. It has to do with you. As long as you've been true to yourself and your values, and you've given your all, there are no justifications required, only learnings for the future. This is what will carry you through the bad weather you experience in life.

What is life for but to explore, to make the most of the short time that you have here? So really it should all be turned around: if you haven't failed, then you haven't tried and therein is the shame; you have failed to make the most of your life and the opportunity you have been given with your existence and consciousness and if you look on failure like that, then, while there still may be short-term hurt, you can move on to the next chapter.

Standing tall will result in some storms; yet the tall tree is also the first to see the sun come up and the last to see it set and the one who most enjoys the midday sun.

Never stop growing!

Dad xx

14. Variety is the Spice of Life

Borneo Jungle
September 2010

I don't notice the leeches in my socks or the insect bites, or how wet through I am. Until we stop to build camp for the night. Until I stop my focus on everything else.

***

The jungle is an unforgiving place. Map-reading is difficult; there is no visible definition in the forest; ridges and streams are equally hidden in foliage. The concentration, driven by nerves and the unknown, is relentless.

Continuously hacking at undergrowth with my parang, watching for what is behind or underneath but always thinking of the next step; giant leaves, branches, rounded, spiked – an amorphous verdant mass to me but each with its own survival mechanisms. One minute my foot is disappearing into a hole, hidden by detritus, the next I'm struggling for balance as I attempt to avoid holding anything for fear of a hidden spike or creature, the next ducking under a web spanning the tree gap in front, a black spider bigger than my hand resting in the middle.

I stop noticing the rain, despite its insistence; the humidity weighs on my shoulders and sticks clothes to my skin like Lycra. Wading streams changes neither temperature nor wetness.

The canopy above intermittently lets direct sunshine through to provide some external reality to this Eden, rays of light piercing the heaviness of the umbrella. Shrieks and whistles bounce around the air above as we move; jungle sirens, but they mean nothing to me.

Woody calls camp late afternoon. 'Remember, avoid older trees for your hammock,' he shouts. Good point, don't want a collapsing tree or branch on me at midnight!

I find two solid-looking ones about the right distance apart and start to clear the area around with my parang. This place is going to be my recuperation and my haven for the next few hours.

A dry and safe place to sleep is the cornerstone of sanity here.

Dry because you are wet the whole time outside your sleeping area. You don't realise how much it rains till you experience it and, while on the move, you are regularly having to cross streams, getting your feet into a permanent wet state throughout the day that gradually makes them disintegrate (literally) over time – something you've got to be careful of, ensuring you're inspecting them each night and then rubbing in large quantities of talc.

Safe because of the number of bugs and animals around. Some of the guys are literally covered in hundreds of mosquito bites. You have to be so careful with your hammock set-up and getting in and out of it. Your sleeping area consists of three parts, the hammock itself, the mosquito net and the tarpaulin. The hammock has to be set up [between two trees] with the feet end slightly higher than the head – counter-intuitive but it stops you sliding down at night. The tarpaulin has to be very tight as the rains can be punishing. You don't want the hammock too close to the ground as the rain can splash so high that it bounces into your hammock!

Underneath you build a tripod to hang your rucksack on – to keep it off the ground and things from crawling in. The same goes for sticks to put your boots upside down on.

The net clips under the hammock and relies on downward body pressure to keep it tight and midge-proof. So you want to get into your hammock (under the net) as quickly as possible without taking in too many animals with you. This is tricky for a number of reasons; the hammock is high and obviously swings. You want to turn off your head torch to not attract too many bugs as you get in and you have to take off your wet boots before you get in and you want to take off as much wet clothing as possible just before you get in.

So the sequence is: light candle and head torch off, boots off on to their sticks while balancing on my 'dry' shoes. I would then typically drop my wet trousers to my ankles and jump on to the hammock, lifting the net and slipping under as quickly as possible.

At the point where I think that I have the net as secure as I can underneath me, I turn on the head torch again; fairly quickly after that, I'd get an idea of how many animals there are on the inside. I have learnt I can clear up a lot of these by reading. The light on the page attracts the bugs and I can then kill them. My book is littered with animal relics!

Regarding other animals, the obvious one is the leech. Daily we would rub super-strong Deet into the tops of our boots. Especially after a burst of rain, leeches would be everywhere and they can get in anywhere. The funny thing is that while the idea of this rubbery suction pad gorging on your blood is repulsive, you often feel little more than an itch or small irritation and often they have been and gone before you notice. But part of the nightly routine of trying to dry and talc yourself in your little home is to check for leeches. I would find ones on ankles or between toes; they were easy to get off once they had had their fill – they just made a mess.

***

For me, the hostility of the environment was wearing. For the local Iban, it was home. What was a cacophony of noise to me were individual animal calls to them; what looked a potentially hostile plant to me was a medicine or food to them. Bugs that attacked me didn't bother them.

The jungle would take a long time for it ever to become more than a challenge and a battle for me. Time to explore elsewhere…

***

'… habit rules the unreflecting herd.'

William Wordsworth, Ecclesiastical Sonnets,
XXVIII 'Reflections'

'The man whose whole life is spent in performing a few simple
operations, of which the effects, too, are perhaps the same …
generally becomes as stupid and ignorant as it is possible for a
human creature to become.'

Adam Smith, *The Wealth of Nations*

'You only realise, when you travel, the limits of your horizons.'

My diaries, Chile 1996

My Dear Kate,

You will often hear people say (especially as they get older) that time flies by; the reason for this is simple. The more every day, every week, every month is the same, the more everything merges into one undifferentiable mass; there's no perspective. It's like pulling a sled across a never-ending white mass of ice versus climbing a mountain where every movement and every view is different. In the former, days merge in a colourless montage; in the latter, there's something new all the time, your brain and your body are alive and in tune, focused on the details of the task at hand.

When you look back at your past, the years will merge more and more but one thing is certain: if you're lucky, you'll only be able to recall a few memorable things each year. They will be the momentous things not the mundane, good and bad. But they will provide the definition to your existence when you look at it, the mountains that stand out from the plains of day-to-day living.

We all need routine in our lives; we cannot live in a permanent state of flux. The familiarity of family and friends or the recognition from the local shop or pub are very comforting. The stability of the roots in our lives helps especially in times of personal uncertainty.

The problem comes when routine soaks up the majority of our time, when routine becomes so default that it is done without thinking, a life of habit and ritual, as Wordsworth comments. Then does definition in life disappear.

Too much routine leads to a mindset that is, by definition, more set in its ways. Just as, if we go to the gym and only work on certain machines all the time, we will only exercise those specific muscles, so the brain gets locked into habits, attitudes and ways of doing things.

The more routine, the more we are prone to park our brains. Our working life, where we typically spend the bulk of our waking hours, can get taken over by it. Adam Smith's quote is tough but it is hard to argue with the logic. It is important not only to find challenging work, but to challenge that work.

This is why variety in life is so important; for relationships, work and for personal well-being.

Variety in life adds not only perspective but dimension. Which of these has more meaning – a meal from a tin or a Michelin-starred restaurant? It depends, of course. Repetitive packaged food, whatever the hunger level, has to be forced down after a while. But eaten after a long hike, sitting in front of a perfect sunset with friends by a fire? You could be talking about the moment for years to come. Similarly, the restaurant meal might be to celebrate your engagement but, if you're rich, it might be as mundane as a cup of tea. If you have nothing to compare with, the taste has no meaning. Drinking vintage champagne the whole time would be as dull as drinking water the whole time; but fresh water from a stream at the end of a long trek tastes at least as good as champagne on a special occasion. It is events that ultimately have the meaning, while situation adds colour.

Of all experiences, travel provides the greatest variety in life.

You will get to explore the beauty of life in this world as well as its ugliness, its structure and patterns as well as its randomness, its heartlessness as well as its compassion, its smallness and interconnectivity as well as its scale and grandeur. A single plane ride opens up cultures and experiences completely different to our own; from cultures that have survived millennia without exposure to the Eden that is Western consumerism to the influences of different religions on peoples and regions, to the impact of geology and evolution across our planet on how our world has developed. From the crumbling facades and ramparts of communist Cuba to party rule in China to myriad interpretations of democracy across the world; from the complex intricacies of Japanese etiquette to the brutish survival existence of the African wild to the effervescence that is the Carnival at Rio. From an opera in Verona to the Pamplona bull run, from da Vinci to Glastonbury, from Mount Kailash to Jerusalem, these experiences all provide challenges to our perspective and contrast to our existence. They help shine a light on our day-to-day.

From the majesty of the Parthenon to the ingenuity of Petra, from the cave art of Australia to the wonder of the Sistine Chapel, from the origins of Aristotle and Confucius to the killing fields of Cambodia and Auschwitz, from fragments of the adventures of Marco Polo to those of Captain Scott, the journey of our species is all around, our greatness and at times our hubris, our ability to create enormous beauty and achieve incredible feats of endeavour, at the same time as our capacity to destroy and commit foul acts. Personal experience multiplies the impact many fold over words or pictures. From seeing the sign 'Arbeit Macht Frei' or kids scrapping over a rubbish site in India or the splendour of St Peter's in Rome, the emotions triggered by these in person will stay with you for a long time. They bring different scale and angles to existence.

Variety in the smallest things keeps interest and provides colour throughout life. But it is through exploring the variety in the world at large that you'll really get to find appreciation and perspective. It will challenge you to challenge your everyday.

With love,

Dad xx

15. Seek the Guidance of Others

Botswana 2017

It must have been dozing. Out of its hole into the early morning sunshine for a snooze. And that was our luck.

It was all so fast, I'm not sure in what order events happened. Mosa was suddenly off his bike, shouting, more animated than I had ever seen him. Something instinctive had already fired in my body; I had slammed on the brakes and dismounted and was walking my bike backwards before I had time to register what was in front of me.

Panting, every hair on my body on end, every neuron on fire, I blinked away drops of sweat, eyes straining out.

The snake's head was lifting from the ground. 'A ****ing cobra!' my head was screaming. 'I hate ******* snakes!'

I stopped maybe four metres away and looked over to Mosa on the other side of it. I had no idea how either of us had missed it. You could tell he was shaken too. It was at least six feet long, doubled up, and we'd been centimetres away from it.

The head stayed raised.

We stood looking at it for a while and then Mosa said, 'They can spit venom three or four metres,' as if we were in a zoo behind a two-inch-thick glass screen.

Moron! Thanks for telling me. I couldn't believe he was saying this now. I back-stepped the bike even further.

'Let's get out of here, Mosa.' I didn't feel comfortable in its presence, however distant. I cycled a big circle round the bushes to where Mosa was waiting, eyes never leaving the dusty brush in front of my wheel.

We cycled off and pulled up under a nearby mashatu tree. 'So do you have anti-venom on you, Mosa?' I couldn't believe I was asking this question now. How long had I been going into the wild?

He hesitated. 'No, the guides don't carry any.' He looked at me a little defensively.

'So, so what's the process if you or I had got bitten then?' I was getting animated but as much at my own idiocy as incredulity with him.

'So we would get on the radio, and call for a vehicle.'

'And…?' I looked at him.

'And we'd try to catch the snake so they could take it to match the anti-venom.'

'Ah, so there's a hospital nearby?'

He shook his head.

'So…?'

'They would call a helicopter to come for you.'

'And how long would I have?'

'Maybe up to 24 hours.'

I relaxed a bit.

'So I could survive for 24 hours without anti-venom?'

'It depends…' He was looking away now. 'You might need CPR.'

Back at camp, I sat down by the fire pit, energy draining from my shoulders. Getting so close to a live weapon of death felt very different to risks I had seen on my other trips.

Ana came back from her horse safari. 'You OK?' She could tell I wasn't right.

'You're not going to believe what just happened,' I said. I told her the story.

She smiled. 'This is Africa,' she said, repeating the common refrain I had heard from so many out here in the bush.

***

'If I have seen further, it is by standing on the shoulders of giants.'

Isaac Newton

'If you are the smartest person in the room, you're in the wrong room.'

Quoted by Simon Kuper in the *Financial Times*

Kate,

Ana had found a cycling safari at the same place she wanted to go on horseback. 'Sure, I'll come,' I had said without much thought, 'there's a guide for me, right?' I scanned the email – dedicated specialist guide, who would always be carrying a gun with him. Sounded like fun, maybe a little bit of danger but I'm sure they must know what they're doing. And I left it at that.

I guess when I saw the 1930s' Lee Enfield on Mosa's back as I was introduced to him for the first time, it should have been a warning sign. I did jokingly ask if he had just stolen it from a museum, but the fact that he answered it seriously should have given me a clue. I should have been asking more questions. And I should have had my own plan if necessary.

I've been up many mountains now, sailed oceans, and been to many wild places, and almost every time I have been with a guide, or a companion who knew his stuff. As a crewman on the RTW race, I would have felt pretty exposed without a professional skipper – I hadn't followed the long apprenticeships of Slocum or MacArthur when I boarded that boat in Durban.

It is how I have learnt and it is how I've regularly gone about expanding my experiences. I've found that guides give me confidence and support to push beyond what I'd have attempted otherwise.

I've just got back from an ice-climbing trip in Scotland as practice for Peru. I've not done a lot of serious ice climbing but I was going to be climbing grades III and IV on this trip. This is how these grades are classified in the books:

Grade III: Mixed ascents of moderate rock routes; icy gullies; sustained buttresses.

Grade IV: Steep ice with short vertical steps or long pitches up to 70°, or mixed routes requiring advanced techniques.

Seemed quite challenging to me on paper but there's a big difference between leading and following! Richard, my guide, would lead each route and then he would belay me up from above; in other words, I was always on a rope and in theory had little distance to fall were I to slip. A couple of times I felt stuck, completely, in a precarious place with maybe only one 'bomber' hold, as it is called, breathlessly trying to calm myself down and find a way up, unable to find either enough ice to sink an axe into or a rock cranny to wedge in… until finally I would stretch to the limits of everything, it felt, and an axe would sink deep into some ice, beyond where my sight could reach. I would breathe hard into the ice and rock in front of my face and, in forced anger, haul myself up. There were a number of sections like this that I wouldn't even have attempted without that umbilical cord attached to my harness.

Is it 'cheating' to use a guide? Definitely, purists would look down their noses at me on this and I'm sure a number have done over the years! But so what. That rope gave me the confidence to reach beyond any limits I would have mentally defined myself. It fast-tracked my learning and my experiences.

Capability comes down to three things, knowledge, skill and attitude, whether in work or play. Sometimes, like in fly fishing, technique is 80 per cent of the battle; sometimes attitude is all, like in pulling a sled. An expert, like a guide, should have the technical expertise to judge and advise on skill and the experience to impart knowledge; that's their job. If they know you, they can assess effort, too, but really you should be best placed to do this, as long as you can be honest with yourself.

So seek out guides; if they've been there before, they can point the direction. If they've done it before, they can advise on technique or tactics. They can help you get down the experience curve faster and push you to reach beyond where you might have otherwise. They've seen many of the potholes. Good ones are passionate about what they do and generally want to share their enthusiasm, if you are an inquisitive and receptive listener. Of course, there are bad ones too; I've had ones who have treated it just as a job, which it is not.

I was climbing Mont Blanc in 2000 with friends; the others had turned back and my guide wanted to go down too. The weather wasn't great but it wasn't bad and I knew that if we had to turn around, a hut wasn't too far away. So I pushed the guide to carry on. He gave me a typical Gallic shrug and some mutterings in French but turned upwards and an hour or so later we were on the summit. This is the only time I've overruled a guide. It shouldn't be a habit but sometimes you have to call them out or test their motives. Mosa was a decent and earnest guy; he just didn't operate (or his company didn't) to the standards I would have expected. But that was my fault.

If it is for longer than a trip or an experience, then a mentor can be a real help. Someone who has been there before, certainly, so they can give practical advice, but also someone who understands what you're about and can empathise with you and what you're trying to achieve.

I've never had what I would call a mentor, though I have learnt from many different people. I guess that is partially why I have written this book. They don't grow on trees. But I know I would have benefited from one at certain times, particularly during my business career. I have hung on too long out of stubbornness when hope had long since flown out of the door and I'm sure got too blinkered at times, and missed opportunities. Decision-making can be lonely and someone who has been down similar tracks, has gained a few scars and whose advice you trust is worth a lot.

Leveraging and learning off the shoulders of others is how you see further in life. Whether you actually reach those horizons, that's up to you.

Love always,

Dad xx

16. The Virtue of Reality

Nova Scotia, October 2011/
Lovech Forest, Bulgaria, August 2017^{***}

The rain has stopped. The air is heavy and damp; rays of light diffuse through trees and shimmer on leaves, but I do not feel them yet. I like these early moments; the place seems to quieten down when light arrives, and I bask in the warmth and dryness of my sleeping bag for a few minutes. I look over. Steam drifts up from where last night's fire was. Woody is still sleeping. I look at my watch. 5.30. Time to get that water going.

I put on the same damp shirt, trousers and socks from yesterday, the smells of wet smoke well baked into them, and I head off to collect wood. I scavenge small twigs initially, snapping them as I go to check they crack rather than crumble in my hands; and then the same exercise with larger sticks.

There's no such thing as dry here, so I pull out my knife and start peeling wet skins off sticks to create dry shavings and plumes of feathers of wood. I carefully load three of these on top of each other and place my lighter at the bottom. As the feathers flicker with light, a brief satisfaction rises within me but I know it's fragile. I slowly add a handful of twigs, and then another, and finally, with some careful blowing, I can see I've got it going.

Woody brings water up from the stream. 'Morning, Paul.'

*** This is an amalgam of two trips.

'Hey Woody, good night?' I look at my watch – 6.30, one hour to get the fire going. 'Yeah, slept like a log.' He always did. But this is like home for him.

He brings out our bag of flour. 'Pancakes or crepes?' he jokes. He was good at making something edible out of not very much. I line up logs either side of the fire to put the coffee pot on.

The life-giving crackle of the fire and the smell of coffee in the still air wake my senses; they are simple pleasures, but they make that time of the day very special to me. We sit and enjoy the stillness of everything. The forest is not yet fully awake. The stream gently burbles away, making its own way.

Over a couple of fried crepes, I ask, 'Same again today, Woody?'

'Yup, we'll head over to dig some worms on that bank we saw yesterday, and then head for the lake,' he replies.

We are not allowed to trap here so fishing and foraging are our only options. I think of our small taking from yesterday. My stomach is getting used to less, but still growling. I know I'm losing weight. You don't know what the day will bring, even if you know the place. You just know you've got to give it your best. The results are there at the end of each day in the most visible way!

By the time we've cleaned up and got our gear for the day ready, it is nearly eight. The basics of living take time.

We axe branches to make picks to dig for worms in the banks of the stream; some places where animals have been digging are good spots to work, but it is hard and concentrated on the hands and knees just for a jar of bait. Then the hike across the woods and brush to the lake. Then there are the vagaries of the fish.

The lake is still; a slight breeze flicks the top. The sun is starting to dry the air and warm my being. I may even dry out today! I think back to the *Tent Dwellers* book and smile. We are retracing their steps through Nova Scotia back country; they were doing it in slightly more luxury than we are – but they were also a lot more successful at trout fishing! No hunger in that camp!

I had no luck with trout yesterday. I don't know why. I'm no expert but I tried different flies and spinners. I think of the few small fried perch we had for dinner last night. Thank goodness we've still got some rice and couscous left.

'I'll have another go at the trout, Woody.' I get out my fly rod. I'm dreaming of a fresh trout. There should be trout here; where the hell are they?

Woody is already on a float and bait. By noon, it is me zero, Woody ten small perch. I don't know how many casts I have done. My left arm and shoulder ache. Time to switch. We've got to eat.

The rains of yesterday have given way to blue sky. The lake is pristine. Not a soul in sight. Nature has its own rhythm and here we are hustling away just for basic survival. I guess if we could trap or hunt, things would be different.

I cast the float out; it settles, and nothing. I pull in, reset the height and recast. This time, a few minutes later, it starts bobbing and a flick of the rod and I have my first fish of the day at 1 p.m. A three-inch perch. Half a mouthful there, maybe.

At the end of the day we have around thirty, mostly small, perch. We set about deboning them and descaling the skin; Woody can get through them quickly. For me, each one takes time and still has scales on.

Back at camp, the light is fading. I go for more wood and go through the same process to get the fire going, while Woody is getting water and food prepared. Normally I would be ravenous by now, but I know what's coming. It's like dehydrated food on a mountain that you've got to force down. Woody piles a bunch of fried fish in my bowl and I get to work with my fingers. Each one is a low-tasting small mouthful of flesh interspersed with bone. For sure, the calories-out for calories-in don't add up! But what else can you do?

As the night chill settles among the trees, the fire breathes energy back. When I sit in front of it, I can get mesmerised by its flickering warmth; it is the best friend to a man in the wild. We chat for a bit over a hot drink, but tiredness always comes to me early. I love getting into that warm dry haven of my bag and taking in where I am for a few minutes before sleep takes over.

I often think of Proenneke's comment: '*Funny thing about comfort – one man's comfort is another man's misery. Most people don't work hard enough physically any more, and comfort is not easy to find. It is surprising how comfortable a hard bunk can be after you come down off a mountain.*'

The ground is hard but I will sleep like a baby.

***

'To normal people like ourselves living under abnormal circumstances, Nature could do much to lift our thoughts out of the rut of everyday affairs.'

Apsley Cherry-Garrard, *The Worst Journey in the World*

'We have come increasingly to forget that our minds are shaped by the bodily experience of being in the world – its spaces, textures, sounds, smells and habits … We are literally losing touch, becoming disembodied, more than in any previous historical period.'

Robert MacFarlane, preface to Nan Shepherd's
The Living Mountain

Dear Kate,

Virtual reality is incredible. I've walked an imaginary plank a hundred foot up over a gorge that I *knew* was not real and my heart was beating like I was on a rollercoaster.

The quality of virtual reality is becoming barely distinguishable from real life. You can live in your head and in as many and as deep virtual worlds as you like; you can create your own realities. Future generations will have some interesting debates about what is the self and what is reality, when all parts of a body can be replaced or regenerated and parallel 'worlds' exist. That is not for here.

The virtual is already incredible for entertainment and education and will only keep expanding to the limits of our imaginations, but is it good for anything more? When you can replicate all the sights, sounds, even smells virtually, why step outside your headset or your home? For pilots with flight simulators, it is perfect training; better than ever can emergency situations be practised in life-like situations, without risk to life. In games, you can kill and die in virtual worlds and wake up the next morning to go to work.

Yet herein lies the issue with the virtual world – it is not real.

Decision-making has no consequences and, without consequence, there is no meaning.

Our time on Earth is linear; you cannot press stop, rewind or delete in real life. It is the process of conscious decision-making and taking responsibility for the very real consequences that provides colour, dimension and meaning to life (of course, this is why some wish to escape it). You cannot practise falling in love in a headset. You cannot feel the pain of a cut. You cannot replay a bad conversation. You have to deal with them, you have to wake up the next day and figure out what you do next – it matters. It affects your path and potentially that of those close to you.

Rather than practising in the virtual, what about learning from and in the most real place on Earth – nature? Nature is the reality before humans created other ones; it is where we came from, and how we are today is a consequence of our journey in it. We are a part of nature yet the progress of man is making us more and more alienated from it; we continue to plunder from it and invade it for our own purposes, with consequences we ignore or are yet to see. Individually, we are less attached to it and less aware of it.

This plays out in our senses. They were essential drivers of survival, our passage through natural selection, but now they are used more for splashes of colour. We all recognise the beauty of simple pleasures, the smile of a child, the warmth of a fire, the smell of freshly cut grass, the chirping of birds in spring. Such things are all around us, but the birds are increasingly forsaken for mobile phones, nature's smells for perfume, and the stars at night for a TV screen. We all do it; we've all got more important things to do. Or so it seems at the time.

Senses get dulled as a result. You only see this when you meet those who still rely largely on their senses for survival. Watch an Iban in the jungle who can distinguish the cacophony of sounds all around him down to the individual animal or bird, or a tracker in the northern territories following an animal and his ability to spot marks and recognise the smallest disturbed brush, or a local hunter in the African savannah who has to outwit the senses of his prey.

There are large areas of this Earth where the hand of man is distant. From the huge horizons of the oceans to the Antarctic ice, from the parchedness of the Atacama to the floods of the Kalahari, from the mountainous dunes of Namibia to the panoply of the Himalaya, from the wilderness of Alaska to the promiscuity of the Borneo jungle, from the phosphorescent plankton that light up the bows of a boat at night to the power of a herd of elephants at speed through the African savannah, from a sunrise over Uluru to a sunset on a felucca drifting down the Nile. Journeys and experiences through such places fill the mind with warmth and sustenance way beyond their time.

Nature doesn't care who you are. Being out in nature is not dependent on being 'good' at anything or on being something or anything at all. The only thing nature will do, if you push it hard enough, is expose falsehood and vanity. It only deals with reality and truth because it acts as a silent and personal mirror. It provides companionship for those willing to contemplate. As a foil to everyday life, it is the antithesis of the fake and trivial. When you have walked among the giants of the Nepali gods and goddesses, you will tread more softly not only in the hills and meadows of Britain but in its streets too.

Experiencing nature is not from a balcony, but up close. It is about connecting with and letting your senses absorb and infiltrate what's around you; it means committing time to the experience. If you let your senses awaken your mind, it provides real contrast and freshness to your perceptions.

When you return from nature, both your mind and your senses are more awake. You feel more alive and you appreciate the realities of the everyday more, whether that's an intimate moment with a loved one, tuning in to the morning birdsong outside your window, the taste of a Sunday lunch or a nice bottle of wine. Many pleasures come from simple sensual experiences. Many of our memories are treasured and relived through them.

There is no better garden than nature to cultivate your senses and keep a check on reality.

Dad xx

17. Get Good at Getting Better

Manaslu, high camp, 7,400 metres
Midnight, 25 September 2013

A head torch flashed in the darkness, briefly illuminating the icy roof of our tent. My eyes flicked open, my wandering dreams banished instantaneously. Sangay was starting to move towards the stove; Louis was reaching for his head torch. I lifted my oxygen mask. 'Is it time?' I said. The nerves were speaking; I didn't need an answer. I reached down my sleeping bag for my water bottle and inner boots to start the process.

Outside the tent, the air was as clear as Arctic water, the moon lighting the slope in front of us towards an invisible summit. The wind was silent; what relief. The conditions were holding.

I didn't see Damien or PK appear but I didn't ask why at the time; I was focused on getting myself ready, getting my pack sorted and getting my harness and crampons on – incredibly arduous tasks in the cold and altitude. It was welcome to get the 2 litres/minute of oxygen going and to get moving up, partly to settle the nerves but also to keep warm. It was a still night, though, and clear – it was in our hands now...

It was hard going; but I knew it would be. I knew that others would be hurting at least as much. I felt strong because I knew that I was supposed to feel like this. If I kept my head down, didn't make a stupid mistake, I knew

I could do this. That is a great feeling. I had done a lot of apprenticeship for this moment; I was calling in that experience. It carries you through the darkness when your world is limited to the rhythm of breathing into your oxygen mask and that patch of ice in front of your boots that is illuminated by your head torch.

As the sun broke over the horizon, the energy it gave both physically and mentally was inspiring… Then finally in front was the summit ridge. I scrambled on my hands and knees inelegantly up the last cornice of ice, a curved lip shape that has a 4,000-metre drop-off either side, to take a picture or two. The summit itself was a bundle of nerves; it was very exposed. It was only when I got off the lip to a seemingly more stable platform that I started to take it all in. My being felt lighter; I'd made it up an 8,000er and my elation soared in proportion to the view of the Himalayas around. I hugged Louis…

I was keen to start heading down as soon as possible. Phil had set us a target of base camp but a minimum of camp 1 as he was worried about the weather coming in on the 26th [bad weather could lock you in at camp 2 and above but not camp 1]. So as ever the summit was only stage one of the day.

We moved quickly down. As I was descending one steep slope, my stomach started going… I had to get to the bottom of the slope as fast as possible. I rushed down the last few metres to flatter ground and quickly tried to take off my oxygen gear, backpack and down suit. Too late. It was everywhere, the pristine snow stained and my suit a mess. For a minute or two I felt like a child, confused and helpless, the elation of before replaced by this dirty reality.

I regrouped. While I fumbled around, I got frostnip in three fingertips. But I was lucky; the weather was still calm and sunny and I wasn't too far from camp 4… So I could get down there and reassess. I could take off the down, wash a bit with wet wipes and put other layers on. As I left camp, I was in a more buoyant mood as I had rationalised and got in control of my situation. It wasn't pretty, I still smelled, but I was fine. I needed to make it off the hill now – personal hygiene could come later.

I was surprised how long camp 4 to 3 took. I couldn't believe we had made it up those slopes only a day earlier! Concentration was all, the odd stumble unavoidable as a foot went deep into a hole, or a crampon flicked a boot.

We got to camp 2 by 3 p.m. It was getting colder and the weather felt like it was closing in. I would have gladly crashed there but I knew we had to get below the icefall… Going down was hard, hard, hard. Abseiling down some tricky bits, in semi-dark with weak legs, dehydrated and hardly having eaten for over 15 hours… I did the last section on my own in darkness with a head torch. It was easy enough but nonetheless a bit spooky; my mind was quick to play tricks: 'I don't recognise this', 'Have I missed the camp?' … I kept calm. I have seen this before, I told myself. Still doubts niggled in the back of my head. Shadows insist on challenging you and playing games.

Suddenly, over a rise, I saw head lamps! I was nearing my resting place for the night and I was all but safe from any potential weather change. Relief filled me, and a deep contentment. The adrenalin started to flush from my legs to be replaced by a blanket of tiredness. But I couldn't sleep yet; I told myself repeatedly to rehydrate. I got out my bag, started boiling water, got brought some by PK and then later by one of the Sherpas. I could start to relax.

Louis turned up. We were all safe.

***

Twenty-three years earlier…

Kilimanjaro
6 October 1990

'We're here to climb Kilimanjaro,' I replied, and then a few seconds later, 'oh, and go on safari.' The stern-faced border guard was trying to live up to his uniform, flicking deliberately through the pages of my passport. But the faded greens, frayed collars and oversized jacket somewhat undermined his tone. His look didn't change. Clearly, meeting four intrepid guys on their way to attempt the heights of Africa didn't impress. He stamped the passports deliberately and passed them back.

Out in the dimming afternoon bush sunshine, Marc took out a cigarette and we sipped warm Cokes that Nick had purchased from dusty crates at a roadside stall. The warmth of Africa seeped over us.

Our driver roused himself from a plastic chair under a nearby tree. 'Shall we go? Not so far now.'

As the car gradually left the border post behind in a cloud of dust, I started to get a few butterflies. *I wonder what this will be like? Never really climbed a mountain before.*

7 October
*During breakfast, as we pondered heading over to the YMCA to talk
turkey to some guides for Kili, we were approached by a local chap offering
us a trip the same day, picking us up in two hours; five minutes of price
negotiation later and we were off upstairs to sort out our kit.*

He had taken a look at our gear. 'You should rent some jackets and hats,' he said, 'it's cold up there.' He had a gentle smile on his face; he'd clearly seen a few muppets in his time. I looked at my boots and wondered if they'd suffice; *just got to get on with it now,* I said to myself.

I had read, before coming out, an account of climbing the mountain by an eccentric Englishman, who had hired porters to take up cases of claret for sustenance. We had a bag of potatoes and rice on one guy's back and a guide called Augusti.

And so here we are eight hours later at the first hut up the mountain at 2,850 metres... Jim's cards are getting a good airing but it'll soon be too cold to play! What fun this is! Anyway, we are now at the foothills of a big ambition.

After 1,000 metres ascent on the 8th, the diary on the 9th reads:

Boys' level of optimism has completely changed as we await breakfast. I am sitting outside our hut in sunshine. We can see the top of Kili – an amazing sight, covered in snow...

The walk up was long rather than hard but in the heat we decided to take our time and really stock up on water... Kibo hut was right at the foot of the steeper section of Kili at 4,750 mtrs... we went to bed early to try to catch as much sleep as possible before the dreaded midnight call up... [but some late arrivals] kept us awake for I don't know how long. Then 12 came – all too soon.

10 October
We were as lucky as hell – cloudless night and not too much wind. We covered ourselves in as many layers as possible because it was very cold and everyone had said the top was freezing. Augusti kept us going at a fair pace, zigzagging up the mountain across a scree surface – we overtook a number of groups, all of whom seemed to be suffering much more... After three hours, it was getting steep and it was now getting to be a real struggle. We stopped every few minutes to recover breath but it was real hell.

Getting to Gilman's Point, we were very tired, a few headaches but no one was sick. Do we go on (the top of the mountain was a further 2½ hours around the crater edge)? The sun was rising, visibility was getting better and spirits were lifting... we had to keep going.

The views were unbelievable, both on the mountain (down to the crater and ice formations) and the landscape. We reached the peak at 7.15. Marc lit a cigarette he'd carried up for the purpose. We took it all in for a good while…

Was it worth it? We all agreed that it was the most physically demanding thing we'd ever done but the sense of achievement is phenomenal and the view and experience of being 'on top of Africa' also tremendous.

At the end of our day's work – over 12 hours walking – we sit in Hirombo hut [camp 2], exhausted but really contented. It is a hell of a feeling to put the feet up and look at others coming up – in exactly the same position as we were 2 days earlier; but now the tension is gone, we can relax. The satisfaction is immense. We order our first beer for 4 days. Augusti tells us we are four out of only seven to make it up the whole day. That makes it even better.

***

'Be brave. Take risks. Nothing can substitute experience.'

Paulo Coelho, *The Alchemist*

'And I tell you, if you have the desire for knowledge and the power to give it physical expression, go out and explore.'

Apsley Cherry-Garrard, *The Worst Journey in the World*

Dear Kate,

I remember when I was around nine, and I was playing for the junior
football team at school; the coach of the senior team came up to
me one week and asked me if I could play for them on the Saturday
morning. Without really thinking, I stuttered:

'My dad needs me to work on Saturday on the farm. Sorry, sir.'

I went a bit red in the face and shuffled off. It wasn't true. I was scared
I'd mess up and maybe embarrass myself or worse in front of some of
the senior boys.

I'm sure I have done it since too, and you may well catch yourself
saying 'I can't…' as an instinctive reaction. What stops people giving
something a go?

The term 'comfort zone' is the area of activities that I feel
comfortable in or with; this is normally driven by experience, in that
if I've experienced something, I'm more comfortable with it. But
of course this creates a circular argument; if I don't want to feel
uncomfortable, I won't want to experience something new, so I'll
never know if I would have been comfortable with it. In this way
do many people experience only a fraction of what they could and
develop to a fraction of their potential, deriving their belief of what
they can and cannot do by what they have or haven't done to date.

Understanding one's comfort zone is not the key, therefore, it is
understanding this circularity and, as a consequence, being prepared
to break it.

You've done it already, Kate. The first time you went into a ring in
a showjumping competition, under those bright lights, just you and

your pony, family and friends watching from the sides, you must have been nervous. It was quite an exposing situation, but you had practised diligently before, you didn't try to break any records, and you got round. That was a huge deal back then, quite rightly. But now you routinely jump three times as high in national competitions. You haven't had any specific long-term goal in mind but each year you've gradually pushed yourself, trying harder fences and entering harder competitions. You've taken tumbles and made mistakes, but you've looked at them and tried to learn from them. You've literally got yourself straight back in the saddle to jump the fence that just caught you out, so it didn't weigh on your mind and you could come out the next time to take on more.

If someone had said to my nine-year-old self that I would be where I am now, I'd have looked at them quizzically, with a combination of 'what?' and 'why?'. I didn't have a climbing bug in me from a young age like Herzog or Simpson, or a sailing one like Slocum or MacArthur. I have just tried things and then, with the things that have intrigued me, I have tried to see how far I could go. It was a journey of twenty-three years from my first real mountain to Manaslu, without ever a particular destination in mind. And it has been the same in every aspect of my life. I've got good at getting better at things.

The books I reference are of some amazing people in amazing situations. We cannot all be MacArthurs or Cherrys but we can get to places and have experiences we never thought ourselves capable of. Anyone can get from dinghy sailing across the estuary to Atlantic sailing if they have the will. But even stopping after getting to the other side of the estuary, if that was the first time in a boat, can give as much satisfaction and personal benefit as an experienced sailor gains crossing the Atlantic. You and I have now done a bit of sailing together on our holidays. If you wanted to, you could be an ocean sailor; maybe you won't want to be and that's fine. Maybe you don't know, in which case try a bit more and see where it takes you.

Now transpose this thought to every aspect of your life, everything from taking on new challenges at work, learning new skills, reading inspiring or questioning books, meeting different people, travelling to engage new cultures, to doing physical activities that test you in some way.

Our comfort zones are places of relief and security but they can also restrict our horizons. Use yours as a platform and reference, not a limit on scope. What you have done does not define your capabilities; it is the range of your attitude and ambition that defines how far you can go.

Whether you will ever fully understand your capabilities is not the point. It is the exploring that is important. I still keep the image of my nine-year-old self with me; I bring it up when I am minded to say 'I can't'. I try to think of 'why not?' now, not 'why?'.

With love,

Dad xx

18. Find Your Own Mountains

Selected diary entries

To me, life is all about the experiences you have… If something happened to me up one of these volcanoes, family and friends will say I was taking too much of a risk: 'Why can't you just slow (or settle) down?' I don't know, is the answer. These experiences are not in themselves risky; you can make them more risky by being stupid about them. They definitely add dimensions to my life. I will never get to the 'experiences' of Simpson (at least not intentionally) but the travelling I do is a tremendous joy and source of inspiration. Every time I have come back from a trip like this I have felt reinvigorated, really up for taking on challenges at work, really able to put things into perspective, to focus, prioritise, more relaxed about myself, more able to take things on the chin because I am happy within myself.

Chile, 1996

Final packing and goodbye to the guides, then Horst, Suze and I walked down the ice to the air strip that four weeks earlier we had traipsed as Antarctic virgins; such a short time and such a steep learning curve. Isn't this what life should be about? Experiences that push your knowledge and spirit, that expand your understanding of self and your abilities and 'wisdom' (though this is not something you can put your finger on or isolate, it develops over time with all such experiences). The four weeks seemed an age, an intensity of experiences to be treasured, remembered and built on. Deeper inner strength and calm I find always on these journeys.

Antarctica, 2005

You have to have something to return to, some waypoints in your life. Cherry was young and he found in the companionship and simplicity of life in Antarctica a purity that could never be repeated. As a result, he spent much of the rest of his life looking back. My antics are by comparison playschool, but that is not the point for me. I have spent my life pushing that envelope bit by bit, challenging my comfort zone and hopefully expanding my horizons. That is the crux of why I do these things. In this small way, I expand my understanding of myself and push my capabilities, knowledge and confidence to take on whatever life has to throw at me round the next corner. Although I believe life is a journey, I am not directionless or rootless. You've got to have those firm foundations in your 'normal' life, in your family and friends, to make the comparisons with such trips worthwhile. You've got to have things you want to get back to. These trips provide the relief and contrast, they don't replace.

Round the World Sailing, 2007/8

***

'I went to the woods because I wished to live deliberately, to front only the essential facts of life, and see if I could not learn what it had to teach, and not, when I came to die, discover that I had not lived.'

Henry David Thoreau, *Walden; or, Life in the Woods*

'Life is never made unbearable by circumstances, but only by lack of meaning and purpose.'

Viktor Frankl, psychiatrist and Holocaust survivor

***

My Dear Kate,

So why do I climb or go into the wild?

Joe Simpson, reflecting on his many near misses, wrote:

'Far from avoiding the trials of life, the danger enables "ordinary life" to be seen in a true perspective, to be appreciated and cherished.'

Art Davidson, reflecting on his epic winter summit of Denali, wrote:

'I returned from our ordeal with a greatly enriched love for life. I came to cherish a lot of things I'd previously taken for granted. Just being alive meant more than ever before.'

It can be easy to lose perspective in 'ordinary life', to get lost in a routine and reactive lifestyle, to take life for granted, as Davidson says; to not appreciate life. The Ancient Greeks talked a lot about life's fragility, because it was ever present, but in modern life we are increasingly abstracted from it. Not so in the wild.

The wild is the foil to everyday life, its mirror, just as it is to the individual. It shines an honest light, a great leveller. Facades and graces mean nothing. It can be capriciously harsh and unpredictable; for sure, it demands respect and attention. At the same time, it is astonishingly beautiful, its complexity disarming, its enduring majesty spiritually energising and, when I have spent time at its heart, it has yielded experiences that have been huge influences on my life.

The combinations of distance from the everyday with exposure to the elements, the physical challenge with the mental, the focus on goals with the need to listen to my senses and the environment around, executing the planned with dealing with the unplanned, the personal responsibility alongside a reliance on my fellow journeymen, the starkness of choices with the need to make decisions, the tests on values with the exposure of character, the perspective on risk together with context on failure, these have all played their part.

I have been on journeys, in work, relationships and of course in my travels and adventures. I have gone from dinghy to ocean yacht, from picnic on Snowdon to oxygen on Manaslu, from bushcraft in Dorset to Borneo jungle, but not by any particularly adventurous routes, and none of them extraordinary.

I've got good at getting better at things, by gradually pushing boundaries, challenging and learning; and thereby, I've got better at being me – knowing myself, understanding what's important to me, being clear on my values and principles. The wild has been my companion and my stimulus on my two journeys; in particular, the internal journey I have been on. I have come a long way from that shy, risk-averse teenager.

The wild has been my stage, my school and my muse. It is what has put a fire under my appreciation of life.

On a mountainside when I am in that zone of focus, life slows to microseconds and time becomes an eternity; at that point, then do I feel really alive, my senses, mind and body working in acute harmony. Where to put the next hand- or foothold has the deepest significance because the consequences are so real. It teaches the link between personal responsibility, decision-making and meaning. The more invested I am, the more meaning I find. And so it is throughout life.

It is the difference between being in front of Thoreau's mast and being below deck. Sometimes that means standing in the face of a gale, but the tingling cheeks, squinting eyes and chilled fingers will scream 'I'm alive'. This is the virtue of reality.

It is not about 'escaping' modern life or building an alternative reality, but about building an appreciation of it. It makes all of life more real and tangible. It helps me 'appreciate what I have', as I said in Antarctica, and understand what is important in life – to me. That is significant; it helps me refocus on what and who are the meaningful, and defer the noise and the fashionable; and in focusing on the meaningful, I find renewed meaning.

If you appreciate life, you value it; and if it is precious, you want to squeeze it for all its worth. You want to learn, grow and explore what there is out there and in you. Yet how many of us lose sight or purpose when in the featureless plains of routine? If days disappear into weeks and years, life goes faster and significance disappears; it gets harder to find fulfilment and definition.

The less you experience in your life, the less you will get out of it. You can go through life in an unchallenged and unchallenging bubble to try to diminish risk or uncertainty, or you can go out and experience it, whether in work, play or relationships; it is through those experiences you have, and the memories, knowledge and learning that you thereby derive, that life reveals itself in its true colours. The more you do, the more life holds for you; it becomes a virtuous circle.

Meaning to life starts from the basic principle of believing you are a free agent and accepting responsibility for your actions. Maximising it comes from leading this virtuous circle of expanding horizons, internally and externally. The tracks you make, the vistas you look on, the people you journey with, all elevate life. As I said in Antarctica, such journeys are an 'intensity of experiences'. They are real life distilled, clarified and raised to a higher plain. The body, the senses, the mind come alive.

So challenge routine and challenge the virtual; seek reality in all you do. Seek people who challenge you and make you a better person. See change as opportunity; don't shy from taking a chance but also remember that she who has never failed has never tried. Listen only to experts and those who care deeply for you. The rest is noise.

Start a scratch map of the world, not to tick things off, but to remind you of what there is left to do and what there is left to learn. Seek colour and dimension in your life, and whatever paths you choose, pursue them with a passion for life. Keep an open mind and heart. Explore! There are always new horizons. As the sun sets on one, it rises on another. You can always find the sun to lift any shadows in your soul.

Be true to yourself and your values; they are your anchors in the storm and the light on your path.

Life is a journey of self-discovery; you start and you finish with nothing. What happens in-between is up to you; that is the challenge and the joy of your existence. The early chapters of your life are already written. From now on it is blank and it is yours to write.

Remember that each paragraph, each chapter, you get the chance to write anew. Build on your past and your experiences but always look forward.

My greatest wish for you is this: that when you look back at your life, you feel it has been *'worthy of the contemplation of [your] most elevated and critical hour'*. To do this, you don't need to climb mountains and you don't need to build your home on Vesuvius, but you will need to find your own mountains in life. Otherwise, you will get lost in the foggy plains of time.

I wish you all good fortune and love as you write your own story. I will watch keenly, I hope share more stories with you, and be there as you need me.

I conclude with these words from Mahatma Gandhi:

'Live as if you were to die tomorrow. Learn as if you were to live forever.'

Good Luck!

My love always,

Dad xx

Epilogue

Here is the letter I wrote on Everest to you; I am glad of course that you never had to open it, and I hope now its message is redundant.

My Kate,

If you're reading this letter, it means something went wrong on the mountain. I can only apologise to you that I will not be there for you and with you as you grow up. You have been a light and a joy to me as bright as any star. The times we have spent together have always been something I have looked forward to and enjoyed; you brought a balance to my life that improved me as a person and added a new dimension to my existence. Thank you.

You will react to what has happened in different ways over time, sadness, maybe anger sometimes, but I hope some pride. I have written up some thoughts for you which I hope will be of use as you grow up; they are unfortunately incomplete but I hope there's enough cohesion there to be of some meaning to you.

Please do not let the fact that I have (presumably) died on a mountain curtail your curiosity or thirst for knowledge. As I have said in those pages, you have one life; live your passions to the full so that when your time comes, you have no regrets. This is what I have tried to do and why I ask you not to feel sorry for me; try to learn from the positives in my life. If some of that can rub off on you, then my life will have achieved much.

You have my love always,
Daddy xx

Selected Author References

Henry David Thoreau (1817–62); writer, philosopher, abolitionist. Thoreau's most famous work is *Walden; or, Life in the Woods*, which I quote from above. Thoreau went into the woods nearby his home town to see what it would take to build a cabin and live as simply as he could. While it describes the simplicity of his existence, it is actually an ode to living and appreciating life. I recommend it!

Apsley Cherry-Garrard (1886–1959); aged twenty-four, he was one of the youngest members of Captain Scott's expedition party to the South Pole. He is most famous for his book, *The Worst Journey in the World*, which describes the whole expedition, but the 'Worst Journey' refers, in particular, to a winter journey in -100+ degree temperatures and permanent darkness to collect some penguin eggs for scientific research. He doesn't qualify for the last five to pull the last sled to the Pole, so is left to be part of the search party the next spring. An incredibly powerful and poignant book.

Joe Simpson (b.1960); climber and writer. Simpson's most famous book is *Touching the Void*, which is such an epic story you'd have thought it was make-believe. He went on to have further close scrapes and he reflects much on this and why he climbs in his book *This Game of Ghosts*. I read this travelling in Chile and it provided a lot of stimulation for my mind and diary on the way.

Dame Ellen MacArthur (b.1976); MacArthur has achieved many firsts in sailing. At twenty-four she was the youngest to take part in the solo round the world race Vendée Globe, and she came second. This feat is described in *Taking on the World*, which I quote above. It describes her journey from a child fascinated with the sea to completing the Vendée. It is worth reading to share this journey, remarkable as it and she is. In 2005, she broke the world record for the fastest circumnavigation.

Captain Joshua Slocum (1844–1909); he was the first person to solo circumnavigate the world. Fifty-one years old when starting it, it was a 46,000-mile journey and took more than three years (versus MacArthur in 71 days!). He describes the trip in his book, *Sailing Alone Around the World*; it's a beautiful book, simply told.

Maurice Herzog (1919–2012); he led the French expedition to Annapurna in 1950 and was the first person, along with his colleague Louis Lachenal, to summit an 8,000-metre mountain; one of the hardest 8,000-metre mountains, too – and without oxygen! It is an epic story, not least for the terrible descent and return, where they had to endure most of their fingers and toes being amputated.

Selected Reading

General

Walden; or, Life in the Woods, Henry David Thoreau
Sapiens and *Homo Deus*, Yuval Noah Harari
Guns, Germs and Steel, Jared Diamond
Atlas Shrugged, Ayn Rand

Adventure

Touching the Void, Joe Simpson
The Worst Journey in the World, Apsley Cherry-Garrard
Captain Scott, Ranulph Fiennes
Annapurna, Maurice Herzog
Taking on the World, Ellen MacArthur
Sailing Alone Around the World, Arthur Slocum
Into Thin Air, Jon Krakauer
Minus 148°, Art Davidson

Acknowledgements

Firstly, thank you to the many people who have shared my journey and provided inspiration, encouragement, fun and advice along the way. You have added so much colour to my life. Writing this book has rekindled memories and stoked reminders of all that I have gained from you.

It is a heartfelt thanks.

With regard to the book itself, I would like to thank John Bond and his team at whitefox for publishing support, and my two principal editorial supports. Andrew Godfrey, who scored and spreadsheeted comments, just as I love. And Ana, my wife and editor-in-chief in so many ways. You know me to a depth that humbles me. Your encouragement when needed and astute comments have made a huge difference throughout this long journey of exploring and writing.